Inspiring everyone to grow

Weeds

Cover illustrations: Photo © Liszt Collection/Bridgeman Images
Back cover illustration: (top left) Royal Horticultural Society, (centre left) Old
Images/Alamy Stock Photo, (bottom left) Smithsonian Institute, Washington,
D.C. (bottom right) The Stapleton Collection/Bridgeman Images

Inspiring everyone to grow

Published in 2021 in association with the Royal Horticultural Society by Welbeck
An imprint of Welbeck Publishing Group
20 Mortimer Street
London W1T 3JW

Text copyright © RHS 2021
Design copyright © Welbeck Non-fiction Limited 2021

A CIP catalogue record for this book is available from the British Library

RHS Publisher: Rae Spencer-Jones
RHS Head of Editorial: Tom Howard
Editorial: Isabel Wilkinson
Design: Russell Knowles and James Pople
Picture research: Steve Behan
Production: Marion Storz

ISBN 978 1 78739 464 3

Printed in Dubai

10 9 8 7 6 5 4 3 2 1

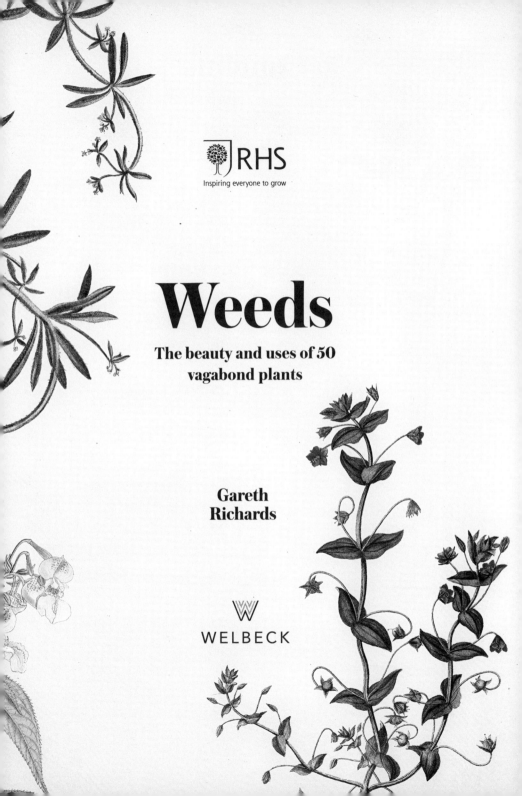

RHS
Inspiring everyone to grow

Weeds

The beauty and uses of 50
vagabond plants

Gareth
Richards

WELBECK

Contents

INTRODUCTION ———— 6

1 *Acer pseudoplatanus* ———— 8

2 *Achillea millefolium* ———— 12

3 *Aegopodium podagraria* ———— 16

4 *Anagallis arvensis* ———— 20

5 *Arctium* ———— 24

6 *Artemisia vulgaris* ———— 28

7 *Arum maculatum* ———— 32

8 *Bellis perennis* ———— 36

9 *Buddleja davidii* ———— 40

10 *Calystegia* ———— 42

11 *Cardamine hirsuta* ———— 46

12 *Chenopodium album* ———— 50

13 *Cirsium; Sonchus; Carduus* ———— 54

14 *Dipsacus* ———— 58

15 *Elymus repens* ———— 62

16 *Epilobium* or *Chamerion angustifolium* ———— 66

17 *Equisetum arvense* ———— 70

18 *Ficaria verna* ———— 74

19 *Galium aparine* ———— 76

20 *Geranium molle* ———— 80

21 *Geranium robertianum* ———— 84

22 *Geum urbanum* ———— 88

23 *Hedera helix* ———— 92

24 *Heracleum* ———— 96

25 *Hyacinthoides* ———— 100

26 *Impatiens glandulifera* ———— 104

27 *Jacobaea vulgaris* —————— 108
aka *Senecio jacobaea*

28 *Lamium* —————— 112

29 *Lemna minor* —————— 116

30 *Malva sylvestris* —————— 120

31 *Matricaria discoidea* —————— 124

32 *Papaver cambricum* —————— 128
aka *Meconopsis cambrica*

33 *Pentaglottis sempervirens* —————— 132

34 *Plantago major* —————— 136

35 *Prunella vulgaris* —————— 138

36 *Pseudofumaria lutea* —————— 142
aka *Corydalis lutea*

37 *Pteridium aquilinum* —————— 146

38 *Ranunculus* —————— 150

39 *Reynoutria japonica* —————— 154
aka *Fallopia japonica*

40 *Rhododendron ponticum* —————— 158

41 *Rubus fruticosus* —————— 162

42 *Rumex* —————— 166

43 *Senecio vulgaris* —————— 170

44 *Solanum* —————— 172

45 *Stellaria media* —————— 176

46 *Taraxacum officinale* —————— 180

47 *Trifolium* —————— 184

48 *Urtica dioica* —————— 188

49 *Veronica* —————— 192

50 *Vicia* —————— 196

INDEX —————— 200

CREDITS —————— 208

Introduction

Fifty botanical vagrants and why we should learn to love them

Weeds are nature's first responders, healing the wounds that man inflicts upon the earth. They valiantly bring life back into even the most polluted land, pushing green shoots of raw ecological power through tarmac and concrete on abandoned sites.

The cheerful daisy in the pavement crack – or even, dare it be said, the buddleia that turns derelict buildings into butterfly havens – countless plants that we dismiss as weeds have amazing powers. Plantains and docks are specialists in helping break up compacted soil. Even those true vegetable vagabonds, Himalayan balsam and Japanese knotweed, are both brilliant bee plants*. Every weed has some redeeming qualities.

When the chips are down, weeds come to the rescue. You cut yourself miles from home on a country walk, there are several weeds you can reach for to help stop the bleeding – and they even have antibacterial properties too. Crops might fail but edible weeds offer sustenance. We might have lost much of our countryside but a select band of plants paint the grey concrete green again. They are a defiant echo of the wild.

In an age of extinctions, weeds offer hope: their very existence is continual proof of nature's resilience. Yet we are so often blind to their beauty. "The notion that a plant is a weed is the most effective barrier for stopping us looking at it closely," wrote acclaimed naturalist Richard Mabey in *The Unofficial Countryside*, first published almost 50 years ago.

Attitudes are at long last beginning to change. You only have to go to the RHS Flower Shows to see how much of a seismic shift there has been in the past half century, since legendary plantswoman Beth Chatto was nearly disqualified for using native plant species (considered by many as weeds) back in 1975. Today such "weeds" as purple moor grass and cow parsley are used in a way that would've been unthinkable back then. Our eyes are slowly opening to the beauty of wild things.

Does being native matter?

Our perceptions are very much a question of time: many of our most-loved wildflowers such as field poppies and cornflowers are technically just as "non-native" as Japanese knotweed, yet because they've been here for many hundreds of years we've grown to appreciate and even love them.

Pinning down the native ranges of weeds is a tricky business. Often they've been around mankind for so long that their precise origins are unknown. Furthermore, the ever-accelerating rate of climate change means that in Britain our definition of native and non-native (one that seeks to freeze our flora into what it was like many thousands of years ago) is looking more irrelevant by the day.

Often the only crime a plant has committed is growing too well. We always want what we can't really have: while we carefully cultivate agapanthus in Britain, it is considered a weed in parts of Australia (it's not native there either). There really is no such thing as a definitive weed. Weeds are much more a perception than a definition.

Only humans make weeds

Nature abhors a vacuum. Bare soil exists rarely in nature, yet we strive to create it by ploughing, digging our gardens, and constructing buildings and roads. If we hadn't created these ecological vacuums, these empty spaces, there wouldn't be nearly so many weeds. They are simply trying to heal our scars on Mother Nature's green skin.

Writing this book has made me realize just how valuable these plants are. If they were all weeded out – which is the logical conclusion to us categorizing them as weeds – our towns, cities and countryside would be immeasurably less beautiful, not to mention almost empty of wildlife.

Wonderful weeds

Weeds are at work everywhere. An unsprayed lawn, full of clover, dandelions and yarrow, will survive downpours better than a pure grass one because its more diverse root structure improves drainage. It also feeds itself (clover makes its own fertilizer by "fixing" nitrogen from the air) and will stay greener for longer in drought conditions.

With wildlife populations in freefall, the choices that gardeners make have never been more important. Learning to use weeds as a tool to direct your gardening is a valuable skill. Creeping buttercup is generally a sign that a lawn is too wet for short grass to thrive. Do you spray and drain it in pursuit of the perfect bowling green, kill the wildlife and make a lot of work for yourself in the process? Or listen to what nature is telling you and turn it into a wildflower meadow studded with beautiful flowers and humming with life?

Possibly the best skill you can learn as a gardener is to recognize seedlings, particularly of weeds, and take a measured approach to whether they're really "weeds" or not. Are they actually weeds here and now, not just on paper? Often the most thriving and beautiful plant combinations in gardens are happy accidents.

Call them by their names

Familiarity really does breed contempt. Even seasoned gardeners know only English names of most weeds. If we called them by their Latin names, would they command more respect? Learn the Latin name and plant family and suddenly a whole new perspective opens up: field bindweed is a *Convolvulus* (related to morning glories), sycamore is an *Acer*, just like Japanese maples. Get to know their names and it's easier to appreciate them.

"The universe is full of magical things, patiently waiting for our wits to grow sharper," wrote Eden Phillpotts just over a century ago. It is a sentiment that still rings true today. The world is changing and many of us are starting to look at our local green spaces differently, valuing what's on our doorstep more than we ever have before. There's so much to be gained from taking time to slow down, look closely and appreciate the small and the wild things in life.

Weeds, those vagrant plants, those wanderers, the uninvited... they have an infinite capacity to heal the earth, to heal our bodies, and maybe just heal our souls too.

*Illegal to plant in the wild, see individual entries

1

Acer pseudoplatanus
Sycamore, sycamore maple

Type of weed:	Tree
Family:	*Sapindaceae*
Uses:	Ornamental
Poisonous:	No

Are we gardeners just a tad xenophobic? Do ecologists,
environmentalists and the like suffer from the sort of nationalism
that leads to blindness in a crisis? If trees could talk, sycamore
would have a good argument for both these points.

Often demonized as a weed tree, an unwanted, invasive alien, in Britain sycamore has had a bad press over the years. Yet there are increasing numbers of people willing to sing its praises. Tough, wildlife-friendly and easily able to live alongside people, sycamore looks like it may well be welcomed in from the cold in the twenty-first century.

As Britain's native trees come under increasing pest and disease threats, what will replace them? Elms have already been lost from the landscape, and ash (*Fraxinus excelsior*) has done a lot to help heal those wounds. Now, as ashes themselves begin to disappear due to ash dieback, sycamore seems a likely replacement candidate because it is fast-growing, easily seeds itself about, and looks at home in the English landscape.

There are voices from some quarters arguing that sycamore is actually a native after all (as suggested by fossil pollen records, although this is difficult to verify). Another way of looking at it is to admit that nature is never still, yet in Britain our definition of nativeness freezes our flora into a snapshot of what it was many thousands of years ago, not allowing for the fact that species' natural ranges change over time. Perhaps sycamore would have got here on its own without help from humans. What's more, climate change is making our definition of "native" less relevant by the day.

Native or not, sycamore is woven into our history. It's mentioned by Shakespeare, the Tolpuddle Martyrs met under a sycamore in 1833 and it has even been spotted in medieval church carvings. Out in the woods, sycamore

behaves exactly like a native tree. It even coppices well and has good wildlife credentials; sycamores support a greater mass of insects than oaks (although not as many different species). In particular they host many aphids, which you could consider the terrestrial equivalent of krill in the oceans: superabundant small creatures that form the all-important base of the food chain.

Let a sycamore tree mature naturally and it can become as handsome as an oak. These large, long-lived trees can grow up to 30m (100ft) tall and are resilient enough to tolerate coastal exposure, cold mountainsides and even severe urban pollution. The tough, pale-coloured wood is useful for everything from musical instruments to cooking implements (it doesn't flavour or taint food).

The palmate (hand-shaped) leaves with five lobes look like the classic maple on the Canadian flag. This similarity is no coincidence: sycamore's Latin name *Acer* shows it's in the same genus as both the famous sugar maples tapped for maple syrup and the Japanese maples beloved of so many gardeners. The family resemblance is also easily seen if you compare their seeds. Technically known by the lovely name of samaras, the winged seeds spin down to earth like tiny helicopters on breezy autumn days. A mature sycamore can produce 10,000 of them a year. This tree wants to help us so badly. Maybe it's time we let it!

{PREVIOUS PAGES} In spring sycamores bear tassels of flowers that are adored by bees

{OPPOSITE} Sycamore (bottom) and its close relative the field maple (*Acer campestre* – top)

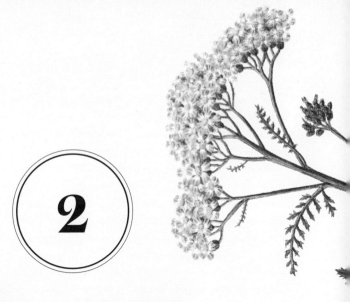

2

Achillea millefolium

Yarrow

Type of weed:	Perennial
Family:	*Asteraceae*
Uses:	Edible, medicinal, ornamental
Poisonous:	No

Yarrow is the quiet superstar of our native flora. A small yet powerful plant, it is used in food and medicine, is good for grazing animals and wildlife, keeps your lawn green in drought conditions and is even good to add to your compost heap.

The usefulness of yarrow means it has been known and loved for a very long time. Its name is rooted in classical antiquity – *Achillea* refers to the legend that the mythical character Achilles, hero of the Trojan War, carried yarrow into battle to help treat his soldiers' wounds. Depending on who you ask, the species name *millefolium* could be from Latin for "thousand leaves" or Greek *myriophyllon* (countless leaves, *myrio* as in "myriad", *phyllon* meaning "leaves").

Rub the leaves or flowers and you get a wonderful warm, sweet green herbal scent. A little like chrysanthemums, it's the scent of a florist's shop. This link betrays the plant family: *Asteraceae* (daisies). Yarrow's flavour is warm, herbal and "green" – somewhere between rosemary, lavender and apples. You can use the flowers and young leaves in both sweet and savoury foods.

Yarrow has many medicinal applications too. It has anti-inflammatory and antiseptic properties which are useful if you cut yourself while gardening or out on a walk in the countryside (hence the old names of woundwort or staunchweed). Do not use while pregnant, however. Other traditional uses include treating everything from colds, flu and UTIs to diarrhoea. The tea is a diuretic (don't drink it before bedtime). Plant or forage the wild species rather than cultivated garden varieties if you want to use this plant for culinary or medicinal purposes.

Back outside, yarrow has other interesting abilities. It helps build soil by accumulating minerals in its foliage. Along with drought tolerance, that makes it a useful component of pastures in dry areas. Grazing animals appreciate the minerals it can provide in their diets, too, and gardeners can make use of them in compost teas or by using yarrow as a compost activator. Yarrow is traditionally called the "plant doctor", as it's thought that planting it next to unhealthy plants will improve their growth. Certainly, lawns containing yarrow stay greener for longer in dry spells.

Many pollinating insects adore yarrow; its flat flower heads make the perfect landing pad for bees and butterflies among others. Having a long flowering period helps too: yarrow starts flowering in late spring and continues throughout summer and into late autumn. Flower heads vary enormously in height depending on the growing conditions, reaching anything from 8 to 60cm (3in to 2ft) high.

More than 50 cultivated varieties of *Achillea millefolium* are listed in the RHS Plant Finder. While the flowers of wild plants vary from a rather dirty white through to pale pink, cultivated varieties come in a wonderful array of colours, including zingy yellows, pinks and oranges through to rich reds.

{PREVIOUS PAGES} Yarrow's strong roots allow it to gather nutrients from the soil

{OPPOSITE} There are numerous cultivated varieties with flowers in many different colours

3

Aegopodium podagraria

Ground elder, goutweed, bishop weed

Type of weed: Perennial	
Family: *Apiaceae*	
Uses: Edible, medicinal, ornamental	
Poisonous: No	

The name strikes fear into many a gardener's heart. Ground elder is famous for being one of the most intractable weeds around. It creeps around underground by means of lengthy but infamously fragile roots – you carefully trace them with a hand fork, right into your precious clump of delphiniums, then *snap*! The root breaks and the trail goes cold. Even the tiniest fragment can regenerate, and frequently does, thumbing its nose at the peeved gardener.

Ground elder, it seems, was likely brought to the UK on purpose. Why? Well, in the days before air-freighted food and medicines for every ailment, ground elder's abundant crop of early leaves found many uses. According to legend, the Romans (what did they ever do for us?) were big fans, bringing it with them to parts of their empire where it's not native (such as Britain) around 2,000 years ago. Many medicinal uses were ascribed to ground elder, principally as a treatment for gout, hence the alternative common name. It was also used as a "pot herb", being added to stews which were a common part of the diet.

These days it has rather mixed fortunes. While ground elder sometimes features on posh restaurant menus, it's often seen as a disappointing wild food by novice foragers. The trick is to harvest the leaves very young. Translucent, picked before they're fully unfurled, they can be added to salads, bringing a hint of carrot and parsley flavour (to which the plant is related). It's a seasonal springtime delicacy that works well with vegetables and fish.

Cook slightly older leaves gently with butter or olive oil and a little water, stirring continuously, until tender. Or try them in curries, soups (especially as an alternative to watercress soup) and as our ancestors did, in stews. Repeated harvests lead to repeated flushes of fresh growth, making this a sustainable perennial vegetable for wild gardens, and one that grows well in the shade.

Ground elder's basic form is a mat of underground roots, sprouting a carpet of lush green leaves around 10–25cm (4–10in) high.

One study indicated that a single plant could cover an area of 3 square metres (32 square feet) in a year under favourable conditions!

Pretty white heads of flowers up to 1m (3ft) tall emerge in June. They look delightful, about halfway between cow parsley and common hogweed in terms of chunkiness. These blooms help give ground elder good wildlife credentials, providing food for everything from bees to beneficial parasitic wasps whose larvae prey on aphids and other garden nasties.

Despite its common name, *Aegopodium podagraria* is unrelated to elder. Its family is the *Apiaceae* or carrot family, which used to be called by the more descriptive name of *Umbelliferae* after their distinctive umbels (like upturned umbrellas) of flowers. Be careful, though: the carrot family is a jumble of edible and poisonous plants. Never eat any wild food unless you're 100% certain of a plant's identity.

A cultivated variegated form (*Aegopodium podagraria* 'Variegatum') is reputedly less invasive than the species, making an attractive and tough garden plant for shady areas. Its light green, cream-edged leaves are an ideal partner for ferns and other woodland plants. However, it can produce seedlings of the green form, so remove the flower heads before the seeds ripen to stay on the safe side. A useful plant for brave gardeners!

{PREVIOUS PAGES} Often hated by gardeners, ground elder has some surprising uses

{OPPOSITE} Pretty, umbrella-shaped flowers show the plant's relation to carrots, cow parsley and hogweed

4

Anagallis arvensis
Scarlet pimpernel

Type of weed:	Annual
Family:	*Primulaceae*
Uses:	Ornamental
Poisonous:	No

A cute and cheeky little plant that creeps
about in sunny spots, throwing out attractive
five-petalled flowers in abundance over the summer.
Scarlet pimpernel has a somewhat mercurial nature,
shifting in shape and colour between sites
and generations.

Sometimes the flowers are orangey-scarlet, sometimes vermilion, pink, white, or even a pure brilliant blue. Sometimes they have rounded petals, sometimes pointed. Botanists have argued for years about which plant family this pretty little flower belongs to, and even whether it deserves its own genus name, *Anagallis*, or whether it's just another loosestrife (*Lysimachia*).

The flowers' opening responds strongly to weather conditions and time of day, closing in dull weather and in mid-afternoon. Hence scarlet pimpernel's plethora of meteorologically themed common names: poor man's weather vane, shepherd's weather-glass, shepherd's sundial. According to countryside lore, they foretell bad weather if they close early.

Scarlet pimpernel's shapeshifting tendencies extend even to its growth habits. It's a tough little thing, capable of growing at different times of year and adapting itself accordingly. As one of our "winter weeds", it is capable of steadily growing through the colder months for a big head start when the weather warms up in spring. Winter plants have dense growth whereas summer plants are sprawling.

Anagallis arvensis has spread worldwide, from temperate places such as the UK to Mediterranean fields and cooler, high-altitude areas in the tropics. In common with many weeds, it simply loves the soil disturbance caused by gardening and farming. However, it's so small that it's rarely much of a problem, as it drapes itself elegantly around the feet of other plants. Just make sure you remove any wayward pieces from dinner plates if it has snuck in amongst your home-grown lettuce!

Several naturally occurring blue-flowered variants exist, but they're tantalizingly rare in cool temperate countries. Research has shown that sunny conditions encourage those with blue flowers (they're much more common in Mediterranean areas). If you love the idea of a blue pimpernel but just can't find one, try *Anagallis monellii*. Slightly stockier and perennial, it bears large flowers for months on end and is a really good pure blue. The species holds an RHS Award of Garden Merit, and several cultivars are widely available.

Scarlet pimpernel's mercurial nature reveals itself again when it comes to the plant's edible and medicinal uses. Some sources say it's toxic, but not very toxic. Others say it's edible, but not very edible. Various medicinal uses have been historically ascribed to the plant, but none seem to have survived the rigours of modern science. The one thing that is certain is that it can occasionally cause contact dermatitis in some people, so if you have sensitive skin, wear gloves when handling the plant. With a plethora of proven edible and medicinal weeds out there, the safest thing to do is enjoy scarlet pimpernel for the visual appeal of its flowers only.

{OPPOSITE} Sometimes blue-flowered variants occur; these are more common in hot places

{RIGHT} Dainty and delicate, scarlet pimpernel repays closer inspection

5

Arctium

Arctium lappa (greater burdock), *Arctium minus* (lesser burdock)

Type of weed:	Biennial/perennial
Family:	*Asteraceae*
Uses:	Edible, medicinal
Poisonous:	No

Burdocks are some of our most interesting, ingenious and useful wild plants. They're used for food, for fun, for medicine; and they even inspired one of mankind's best-known examples of biomimicry – Velcro.

Arctium Lappa.   *Burdock.*

John Frederick Miller, del. 1792.

Pub: as the Act directs, Feb:1,1792, by J.Beu, Nº88, Pater-nofter-Row.

{PREVIOUS PAGES}
Burdocks are striking, vigorous plants
with unmistakable features

{ABOVE}
Like their relatives in the daisy family, burdock flowers have
"compound" flowers made of many individual blooms

Burdock's seed heads (burrs) are covered in tiny upward-facing hooks, and because of the seed heads' spherical shape, they're superbly designed to stick to passing animals or people at whatever angle they brush against the plant. They're so good at attaching they can even hook onto the ridges of skin that make up your fingerprint.

Having been inspired by burdock's curved hooks and how effectively they stuck to his dog's fur, Swiss inventor George de Mestral patented Velcro in 1955. Strangely, it wasn't a hit until NASA heard about it and used it on board their spacecraft to keep objects where they were wanted in zero gravity. All of a sudden, this plant-inspired invention became wildly popular, turning up even in high fashion clothing. The rest is history.

Back down on planet Earth, burrs have been loved by generations of children – like the stems of goosegrass (see page 76) they can be thrown at your companions, and will stick fast to clothes or hair and can be quite a nuisance to remove.

Lesser burdock grows 50–150cm (20–60in) tall, while greater burdock can grow to more than 1.8m (6ft) and has one of the biggest leaves you'll find growing wild in the UK. Soft-textured, wavy-edged and a bit floppy, they make superb natural toilet paper if you get caught short on a walk!

Both species are common in woods and on waysides and waste ground. Greater burdock is what's known as an archaeophyte, having been introduced by humankind in ancient times but growing wild in Britain and other places outside its native range for hundreds of years. Lesser burdock is generally regarded as native to most of Europe (including the British Isles).

Looking rather like miniature artichokes or thistles, the colourful pink and purple flowers offer a clue to burdocks' family identity as part of the *Asteraceae* (daisy) family. Blooming occurs from July to September and the flowers are enjoyed by bees and butterflies.

Although almost the whole plant is edible, greater burdock's thick roots are its main gastronomic attraction. Harvested in autumn or spring, they can be roasted, boiled or even eaten raw, finely sliced with carrot and spring onion in Southeast Asian-inspired salads. They are an important ingredient in Far Eastern cuisine, and the roots are known as *gobo* in Japan, where they're widely cultivated as a food crop. In the British Isles, dandelion and burdock is a traditional drink made by fermenting the roots of the two plants (along with some sweetness from molasses or treacle).

Burdock has many medicinal properties (mainly relating treatment of digestive and skin disorders) and its seeds are used extensively in traditional Chinese medicine. The roots contain large quantities of a carbohydrate called inulin, which is beneficial for gut bacteria and is thought to help stabilize blood sugar levels.

The origins of the word burdock are shrouded in mystery. Some say it comes from the French *beurre* because the large, strong and non-toxic leaves were perfect for wrapping butter (a use that may yet return to favour as more of us seek to avoid using disposable plastic wrap on our foods). Others say it's from *bourre* (meaning wadding or stuffing), referencing the burrs' almost inevitable attachment to wool or fabric. Or it could just be a reference to the burr fruits and the plants' lush docklike leaves. Whatever the name means, this remarkable plant shows us just how useful some "weeds" can be.

6

Artemisia vulgaris

Mugwort, poor-man's tobacco, muggert

Type of weed:	Perennial
Family:	*Asteraceae*
Uses:	Edible, medicinal
Poisonous:	No

Don't be fooled by first appearances. Despite its drab looks and slightly drab-sounding name, mugwort is an ancient and powerful herb that is revered in cultures across the world. It has a remarkable range of uses – ranging from encouraging dreams to enhancing the flavour of soups and stews.

Mugwort's use in Britain and Europe goes back thousands of years. Roman soldiers were said to put it in their shoes to prevent fatigue while marching, and it was one of the nine sacred herbs of the Anglo-Saxons. In medieval times it was used to flavour beer (hence the "wort" in its name) and it was believed to protect travellers from all sorts of trouble, including wild beasts and evil spirits!

The genus name, *Artemisia*, comes from Artemis, the Greek goddess of the hunt, wild nature and childbirth. Although mugwort has been used to help to restore menstrual cycles, it's important not to take if pregnant or lactating (it was formerly used as a homegrown form of birth control). Artemisias are an interesting bunch: they include *Artemisia absinthium* – wormwood – which is one of the main ingredients in absinthe. The well-known herb tarragon is another artemisia, *Artemisia dracunculus.*

Historically mugwort was, and sometimes still is, smoked as a tobacco substitute. Today mugwort is increasingly finding fame as a dream herb. It has a reputation for increasing the vividness and recall of dreams. Other uses include treating parasitic worms, stress, depression and to help with digestive issues.

Sadly, mugwort's usefulness and otherworldly qualities don't translate into physical beauty. It's a rather nondescript plant that likes hiding in plain sight, although once you get your eye in you'll see it everywhere. An upright, woody perennial, it grows 60–180cm (2–6ft) high. Dark green above, bright silvery white below, the leaves are jagged, as if the whole plant has been attacked by scissors. In windy conditions the plants seem to shimmer. Spires of tiny, grey-green, bell-like flowers cover the tops of the plants in summer. Mugwort loves sunny, dry places, such as along roads and footpaths and on waste ground. The taller it is, the more fertile your soil.

You can use mugwort in the kitchen too. The leaves and flowers have a warm, aromatic taste, like a combination of rosemary and sage. Flowers have the most flavour. Mugwort can be used fresh or dried – try it in tomato-based pasta dishes or soups, or with rich meats like goose where its slight bitterness will help temper the fattiness of the meat.

{ABOVE} Mugwort is a curious-looking weed with tiny bell-like flowers and some interesting uses

{OPPOSITE} While not conventionally attractive, mugwort is certainly distinctive

7

Arum maculatum

Cuckoo pint, lords-and-ladies, wild arum

Type of weed:	Perennial
Family:	*Araceae*
Uses:	Ornamental
Poisonous:	Yes

Cuckoo pint is one of our most weird and wonderful native weeds. Everything about it is peculiar, from its strange, hooded flowers to its back-to-front growth pattern. A denizen of dark and abandoned places, it has a slightly sinister air that is picked up in many of its Old English names, such as bloody fingers and adder's root.

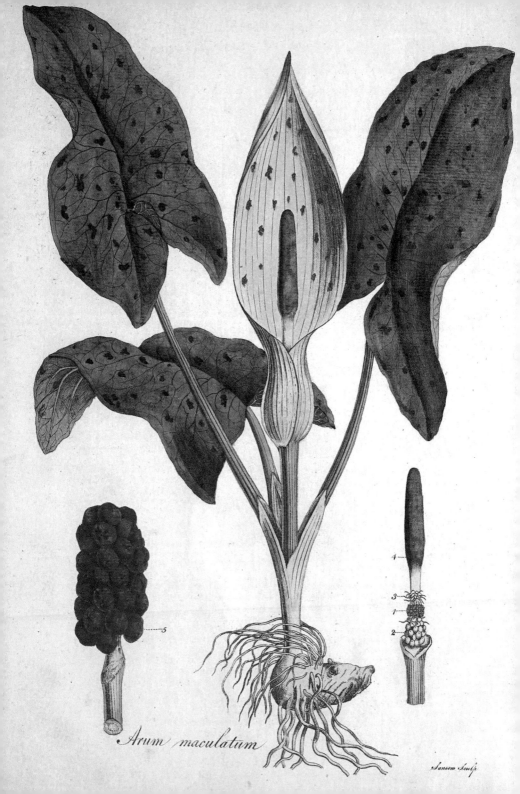

Arum maculatum

Sansom Sculp.

Having very possibly the most common names of any wild British plant – more than 100 are recorded (along with numerous common names in other European languages) – cuckoo pint is a plant that if not loved, was certainly very much noticed by our ancestors. It's distinctive in many ways.

You can instantly tell from its flower that it's in the arum family or *Araceae*. Cuckoo pint is one of Britain and Europe's few native species in a largely tropical tribe, which includes many houseplants such as the Swiss cheese plant, anthuriums and peace lilies. Growing to 30–50cm (12–20in), the clumps of waxy-textured, shiny leaves, sometimes spotted with an unusual dark purple colour, have an exotic look to them despite their hardy nature. Even more strangely, they grow through winter and spring, disappearing completely in summer.

Typical of the arum family, the flower is a large green spathe up to 25cm (10in) high, enclosing a columnar spadix. It all looks a bit vulgar, hence some rather fruity, old-fashioned, common names (naked boys, dog's dibble, cows and bulls, to name but a few). The plant emits a slightly foetid odour that attracts pollinators, mainly tiny feathery-looking flies called owl midges. These then fly down into the flower, past a nightmarish ring of bristles (like a miniature octopus with many arms) and become entrapped at the base of the flower, where they transfer pollen from their previous encounters with *Arum maculatum* onto the receptive female flowers.

As soon as the female flowers are fertilized, the bristles and spathe begin to wilt, rapidly withering away to nothing along with the leaves. All that remains is a cluster of fruit like a huge, elongated scarlet raspberry atop a smooth stalk. The shiny, tasty-looking berries ripen through green and orange to pillarbox red. Don't be tempted by their good looks: they taste foul and are extremely poisonous to humans. Strangely, birds seem unaffected and some species seem to enjoy this colourful wild food.

All parts of the plant are poisonous. If you're a foraging fan, it pays to learn to recognize cuckoo pint because it often grows alongside wild garlic. You can tell them apart because the top of the *Arum* leaf, where it joins the stem, looks like the top of a heart shape, and the leaf veins are branched. If you're still not sure, tear a leaf and sniff – you'll soon tell whether it's wild garlic or not.

If you like the curious look of cuckoo pint but fancy something a bit more garden-worthy, try the Italian arum, *Arum italicum*. It has stunning shiny, marbled leaves and makes a useful winter and spring plant. The variety 'Marmoratum' even has an Award of Garden Merit from the RHS.

{PREVIOUS PAGES} With its glossy leaves and strange flowers, *Arum maculatum* has an almost-tropical air

{OPPOSITE} Don't be tempted by the berries – they are not only poisonous but an irritant too

8

Bellis perennis

Daisy, English daisy, lawn daisy

Type of weed: Perennial	
Family: *Asteraceae*	
Uses: Edible, medicinal, ornamental	
Poisonous: No	

No other plant epitomizes lazy sunny days like the daisy. Open-hearted, simple and joyful, it's one of the best known and commonest wildflowers. Daisies flower pretty much all year round, and they're an especially welcome sight making flowery carpets on lawns and verges as spring hits its stride.

Botanical Latin can sometimes be a bit obscure, but daisies got lucky. *Bellis* means beautiful, and *perennis* refers to its perennial habit (i.e. living for more than a year). Daisies are members of the plant family *Asteraceae* – which is a huge plant family with more than 32,000 species, including garden flowers like sunflowers and echinaceas, along with lots of weeds such as dandelions, thistles and ragwort.

With light green, spoon-shaped leaves, daisies tend to grow in irregularly shaped clumps, mainly in lawns but sometimes in pathways, garden borders and rough grass. They grow to about 8cm (3in) tall when released from the pressure of mowers or trampling feet; otherwise they'll hug the ground at just 3cm (1in) and are very tolerant of trampling and compacted soil. White with yellow centres, the flowers often have pretty pink stains to the backs of the petals. Medieval poet Geoffrey Chaucer wrote of daisies as "day's eyes", referring to the flowers' habit of opening at dawn and closing again at dusk.

Take a closer look, and you'll see that they're not just one flower but hundreds (hence the daisy family is also known as the *Compositae*, which comes from their composite flowers). Each little yellow bobble in the centre is an individual flower, or disc floret. Those on the edge have a petal attached too, and are called ray florets. Daisies' flat, open-faced flowers are the perfect landing pad for all kinds of pollinating insects. What's more, their abundance and long flowering season – almost all year round – makes them an invaluable source of nectar and pollen, especially for bees and hoverflies (whose larvae are great allies to the gardener as they love eating aphids).

Daisies are useful for people too, both in the kitchen and for homegrown remedies. An ointment made from the leaves can be applied to bruises and wounds. Daisy flowers can be gently simmered with water to make a decoction that is thought to ease coughs and other respiratory problems. You can eat them too: try young leaves or flowers in salads.

In a pretty pot, viewed up close on a patio table, even plain wild daisies look stunning. Hardy and easy to grow, double-flowered daisies have long been used in winter and spring bedding displays. Some pretty cultivated varieties such as the Rominette Series are available in red, pink and white. However, like all double flowers, they have less wildlife value because they contain much less pollen and nectar than their wild, single-flowered kin.

If you love daisy flowers but want a more delicate plant, try the Mexican fleabane, *Erigeron karavinskianus*. It has incredible flower power and will happily seed around walls, paths and borders. The pretty white and pink flowers are very similar to the lawn daisy, but the plant has a more elegant form and is great for pollinating insects, too.

{PREVIOUS PAGES} Wild daisies are white with pink petal tips

{OPPOSITE} Cultivated varieties of daisy come in many different forms and colours

Tab. 29.

Bellis hortensis rubra flore Tournef. 491. Bellis Hortensis Linn. Spec. Pl.
1249.
Ical. Margaritina rossa doppia. Gall. La Paquerette, ou petite Margueri.
w

Buddleja davidii
Buddleia, butterfly bush

Type of weed: Shrub	**Uses:** Ornamental
Family: *Scrophulariaceae*	**Poisonous:** No

It's a shame buddleia isn't native to the West; if it were indigenous, we might appreciate it more. Unlike humans, butterflies are pretty much unanimous in their approval, hence the plant's other common name of "butterfly bush".

Buddleja davidii hails from Himalayan mountain screes in China, which explains its love of growing in the rocky ballast of railway tracks and its ability to get a foothold in even the tiniest crack in buildings. It is a star plant for creating wildlife habitats from cracks in bare concrete on abandoned sites where buildings have been demolished.

Pollinating insects, especially butterflies, adore buddleia. "It is always top of the list of most commonly used nectar sources in our Garden Butterfly Survey and lives up to its alternative name of the 'Butterfly Bush'," says wildlife charity Butterfly Conservation in its policy statement on buddleia.

Sometimes people criticize non-native, "wildlife-friendly" plants for providing only pollen and nectar, and not supporting insects through all stages of their life cycles. However, in a now-legendary 30-year study of garden wildlife in the UK, pioneering scientist Dr Jennifer Owen singled out buddleia as a larval food plant for 18 native moth species. This is a pretty incredible endorsement from our indigenous wildlife, seeing as at that point it had been in the country for only about 60 years. Her husband Denis, also a scientist, wrote: "No native or introduced plant produces flowers that are so attractive to butterflies and other insects... The shrub is in every sense a useful introduction, exploiting a previously unfilled niche... it [is] a welcome addition to the British flora."

Buddleja davidii is a medium to large shrub or small, multi-stemmed tree, up to 5m (16ft) tall and wide. Its slim, oval-shaped leaves have pointed tips and white undersides. Long, tapering flower spikes of scented flowers appear in late summer and early autumn in every shade from white to pink, mauve, blue, magenta and purple. Some even veer towards dark red, and these are particular butterfly favourites.

Buddleias are much loved by gardeners: there are more than 200 cultivated varieties of *Buddleja davidii* (9 have the Award of Garden Merit). So why does such a pretty and wildlife-friendly plant have such a weedy reputation? Well, there's a seedy side to buddleia. A mature bush in full pelt can produce three million seeds a year and invade precious habitats such as chalk grassland.

Interestingly, in gardens buddleia doesn't seem to be that weedy. Gardeners tend to trim off the flowers as they fade: this extends the flowering period and also prevents self-seeding. Buddleias do love to be pruned: pruning hard every winter keeps the plants smaller and more compact. Their seeds are thought to ripen only the spring after flowering, so winter trimming should curb the plants' invasiveness too.

{BELOW} With large, attractive flowers and a pleasant scent, buddleia blurs the line between garden plant and weed

10

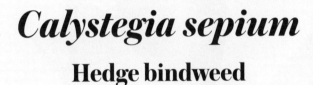

Calystegia sepium
Hedge bindweed

Type of weed: Perennial	
Family: *Convulvulaceae*	
Uses: Ornamental	
Poisonous: If eaten in large quantities	

Look closely at hedge bindweed: its luminous
white, trumpet-shaped flowers, twining stems
and pale thick roots. It's *beautiful*. And terrifying.
It smothers other plants and drags them to the
ground, like something that belongs in a science
fiction movie – or, at least, the tropics.

Despite its exotic air, this is a hardy European native. Those pale, fragile yet powerful roots can penetrate as much as 3m (10ft) below ground; individual plants can live for 50 years and climb for many metres up trees and fences. Stems pop up all over the place, forming huge colonies. They're even more incredible for the fact that in winter they entirely disappear below ground.

Hedge bindweed twines anticlockwise and has mid-green, heart-shaped leaves. It rapidly spreads horizontally, making carpets of leaves, until it finds something to climb up. Then it really romps away, cheerfully adorning fences and waste ground with its beautiful pure white blooms.

Field bindweed (*Convolvulus arvensis*) is a smaller plant with fragrant and pretty candy-pink flowers. Its beauty belies a mischievous nature: it is a great smotherer of other plants. In some areas it is known by the descriptive common names of "devil's guts" or "cornbine". Black bindweed (*Fallopia convolvulus*) looks superficially similar but is quite unrelated, being in the knotweed family, which is easy to spot when you look at its flowers.

One of hedge bindweed's much better-behaved cousins that you might find at the garden centre is *Convolvulus cneorum*. This is a pretty little shrub with bright silver leaves and typical bindweed flowers. Other members of the same plant family (*Convolvulaceae*) include morning glories and sweet potatoes.

Controlling bindweeds is difficult. Dig deeply and thoroughly, removing every trace of root.

Unfortunately, bindweeds can regenerate from even tiny fragments of roots and they break easily as you remove them. You can put them to work (get your revenge) by soaking them, along with any foliage you pull up, in a bucket of water. They'll die, and as they break down they'll make a liquid feed for your plants.

Alternatively, just keep pulling off the top growth every time you see it emerge from spring to autumn. This will eventually weaken the plant. This is one *never* to add to the compost heap, as even the tiniest fragment of root can regrow.

Some gardeners have learned to appreciate hedge bindweed's rampant beauty. When it was time to revamp the flower borders at Waltham Place (a delightfully thought-provoking garden in Berkshire), owner Strilli Oppenheimer insisted it was kept, even building wigwams for it to grow up!

{ABOVE} Field bindweed has a delicate appearance and fragrant flowers that belie its weedy tendencies

{OPPOSITE} Hedge bindweed's beautiful trumpet-like flowers show its family relationship to morning glories (*Ipomoea*)

11

Cardamine hirsuta

Hairy bittercress, land cress, lamb's cress

Type of weed: Annual
Family: *Brassicaceae*
Uses: Edible
Poisonous: No

A tiny, edible plant that's big on flavour, hairy bittercress
is a super-speedy weed that likes to live fast and die young.
Looking rather like miniature watercress, it often hitches a
lift into gardens by growing inside the pots of other plants at
garden centres. Its exploding seedpods can fire seeds almost
1m (3ft) into the air. This is not a plant that hangs around.

{PREVIOUS PAGE} The leaves of this weed have a hot, peppery flavour

{LEFT} Closely related, wavy bittercress (*Cardamine flexuosa*) is another edible weed

Hairy bittercress grows from a rosette around 10cm (4in) across – all the leaves and stems arise from a central point. The leaves are pretty divided with almost circular leaflets; generally plants grow to about 10cm (4in) tall, up to a maximum of 20cm (8in) when in flower.

The resemblance to watercress in both looks and taste is not a coincidence. Both plants are members of the cabbage family (*Brassicaceae*) alongside other pungent yet tasty plants including mustard, cress, wasabi, horseradish and wild rocket. Its small white flowers offer another clue. Look closely, and you'll see that it has four-petalled flowers. These were likened to a crucifix by early botanists, hence the family's old name of *Cruciferae*. Have a look at wallflowers, aubretia or oilseed rape, and you'll see those distinctive four petals.

"Hairy bittercress" sounds revolting: eat a whole handful at once, and it will be. However, just like its cousins rocket and mustard, its sweet and peppery flavour really shines when mixed with plainer leaves such as lettuce. For an ultimate weed salad, gather in early spring with chickweed and ground elder shoots. Harvest over the cooler months from October to May for the tastiest, most tender leaves.

In common with other strongly flavoured but healthy leaves, a salad dressing with some sweetness – from honey or maple syrup, for example, along with a dash of acidity from lemon juice or cider vinegar – works wonders. If the flavour is too strong, use it as a free garnish, just like a wild-foraged version of supermarket cress. Those strong, punchy flavours are due to the presence of compounds called glucosinolates; research indicates that these have anti-cancer and anti-inflammatory properties. The leaves also contain lots of vitamin C and minerals.

Hairy bittercress is found all year round in gardens, allotments, fields and other sites where the soil is disturbed regularly. Occasionally it grows in walls too. Sometimes it's confused with wavy bittercress, *Cardamine flexuosa*, which is to all intents and purposes just a bigger version of hairy bittercress which you can eat in the same way. These punchy wild greens are wonderful for bringing variety into our modern diets. The same could be said for many weeds: if you can't beat them, eat them. You might just enjoy it.

12

Chenopodium album

Fat hen, lambsquarters, goosefoot

Type of weed: Annual	
Family: *Amaranthaceae*	
Uses: Edible, medicinal	
Poisonous: No	

One of the world's most widespread weeds, fat hen grows on every continent except Antarctica. But is it actually a weed? The answer to that question depends upon who you ask.

Fat hen could be called our native version of quinoa. Along with quinoa, spinach and beetroot, it is part of the amaranth family or *Amaranthaceae*, which contains many edible and useful plants. Its genus name *Chenopodium* comes from the Greek words for goose and foot, referring to the shape of the leaves; the species name *album* refers to the distinctive silvery-grey young leaves, particularly on seedlings.

In common with lots of weeds it will adapt itself to the conditions (a trait known as morphological plasticity). Late-germinating plants in poor dry soils can grow just a few centimetres high and complete their life cycle in just a few weeks. When conditions are good and seeds germinate early, it can rocket up to 1.2m (4ft) or more, making lush green canopies of fleshy, soft-textured leaves. The flowers are individually tiny but are arranged in prominent clusters along the centres of the stems. They soon ripen to become greyish bobbly masses of what are technically fruits.

Look closely and each fruit is a tiny green star, made of five segments. Each segment contains a seed. These are edible and nutrient-rich, although rather small. In parts of India, fat hen is known as *bathua* and is cultivated for both the leaves (used in the manner of spinach) and the seeds, which are used in breads and rice dishes.

Sadly, elsewhere, it is mainly birds who appreciate this largely forgotten plant. It is an important source of food for wild birds, particularly as fat hen's resilience means it is one of the most abundant weeds in modern farming. As the name suggests, domestic birds appreciate fat hen, too. The leaves are a source of iron, protein and calcium. If you fancy trying it for yourself, cook the shoot tips and young leaves as you would spinach and serve on toast with a poached egg or as a side dish.

Fat hen is a greedy plant. It loves nutrient-rich habitats and is a frequent weed around manure heaps. You can use it as a handy indicator of your soil's fertility: large lush plants mean you have rich soil – if the fat hen in your vegetable patch is small and weedy, it could well be time to apply some fertilizer and compost.

The best form of control is to eat it, although don't harvest from plants growing around manure heaps because they can accumulate harmful levels of nitrates. Otherwise, hoe off small seedlings or uproot more established plants. As long as they haven't set seed, they'll be a valuable addition to the compost heap. Just beware that the seeds can be incredibly long-lived; they've even been successfully germinated after being uncovered on an archaeological site 1,700 years old!

{PREVIOUS PAGES} Fat hen's nutritious seeds are eaten in parts of Asia

{OPPOSITE} Despite their small root systems, these plants grow fast and can become rather large

547.

Chenopodium album L.

13

Cirsium;
Sonchus

Creeping thistle, spear thistle, marsh thistle, sow thistle and others

Type of weed:	Perennial, biennial, annual
Family:	*Asteraceae*
Uses:	Edible, medicinal, ornamental
Poisonous:	No

You might think that thistles are a prickly
nightmare – no good for man or beast –
but you'd be wrong. Some are edible to us
(including their close relatives cardoons and
artichokes) and many are important food
plants for bees, birds and butterflies.

Thistles have certainly had a bad press over the years. Two of the five species listed by the UK's Weeds Act (passed in 1959 and still current legislation) are thistles: the creeping thistle *Cirsium arvense,* and spear thistle, *Cirsium vulgare* (in North America these are known as the Canada and bull thistles respectively). So this native, wildlife-friendly duo are officially true vegetable vagabonds.

It's interesting that this legislation was passed in an era when farming was increasingly viewed as a war on nature, to be won with ever more machinery and chemicals. Thistles aren't much of a problem in traditional hay meadows, but they are in the intensively grazed systems that became much more common in the post-war era. More than 97% of our hay meadows are gone, as is so much of our wildlife. As we are realizing today, at our cost, it's generally much better to work with nature, rather than against it. These "weeds" are there for a reason, and they always have something to tell us. Thistles are nature's way of breaking up compacted soil, and ensuring that even overgrazed pastures provide some nectar for pollinating insects.

Our wild thistles largely belong to two tribes: purple-flowered *Cirsium* (creeping, marsh and spear thistles) and yellow-flowered *Sonchus* (sow thistles). All have deep green leaves, varying amounts of spines and petal-less flowers. Heights vary from 20 to 150cm (8in to 5ft) depending on species and growing conditions.

They are members of the daisy family *Asteraceae* (see daisies, page 36), and their composite or compound flowers produce plentiful nectar and are really accessible to pollinating insects. In fact, according to one study, marsh thistle (*Cirsium palustre*) is one of our top five best floral resources for pollinators measured in kilos of nectar per unit area per year; along with heather and white clover, it provides 50% of the national nectar provision. Birds such as goldfinches and linnets love thistle seeds, and sometimes line their nests with thistledown (the delicate, parachute-like pappus which thistles surround their seeds with to help them disperse).

Of the sow thistles, the smooth sow thistle (*Sonchus oleraceus*) is the most useful. It's a much-loved winter and early spring green, especially in Italy, where the tender young shoots are eaten in salads or served cooked with olive oil and lemon juice. Rich in vitamin C, beta carotene and protein, the plant also contains vitamin A and calcium. Luckily its name is justified – it's barely spiny at all, and the young leaves are spine-free. If you don't fancy eating it yourself, it makes great food for chickens, rabbits or pigs (hence the common name).

Cirsium vulgare, or spear thistle, is the floral emblem of Scotland and one of the prettiest of the wild bunch. Inside the garden, their relative plume thistle *Cirsium rivulare* 'Atropurpureum' is a trendy maroon version that is much loved by gardeners and often seen at flower shows.

Perhaps the biggest fans of thistles are painted lady butterflies. They visit European gardens on their incredible migration, a journey of 24,000 km (15,000 miles) that can stretch from Africa to the

Arctic Circle, and their caterpillars can decimate stands of creeping thistle – as the founders of the pioneering wilding project at Knepp Castle in Sussex discovered. Just when their grounds were being overrun by the prickly weeds, an invasion of butterflies saved the day. It serves as a parable for aspiring organic gardeners everywhere – hold your nerve and nature *will* find a balance.

{PREVIOUS PAGES} Purple *Cirsium* thistles are nectar-rich and great for butterflies

{ABOVE} Yellow-flowered sow thistles (*Sonchus*) are much less spiny

14

Dipsacus

Dipsacus fullonum (wild teasel), *Dipsacus sativus* (Fuller's teasel)

Type of weed:	Biennial
Family:	*Caprifoliaceae*
Uses:	Ornamental
Poisonous:	No

Statuesque. Ethereal. Unique. Ever-changing in form and colour, teasels are some of our most distinctive wild plants and they deserve to be more widely grown by gardeners. The description "architectural plant" is overused, but teasels fully deserve it.

These tall, rather gothic-looking biennials look like they might have evolved on the set of a Tim Burton film. Every part of the plant has a sculptural quality and is armoured in one way or another. Even the surfaces of the long, tapering light green leaves bear numerous prickles. These stalkless leaves grow opposite each other, their bases clasping the plant's central stem, collecting rainwater in mercurial beads. Historically, this water had all sorts of magical uses associated with it, and was thought to have rejuvenating powers.

The plants themselves have a something of a mercurial quality too, shifting in form and colour across the seasons. In their first year they form a flattish rosette only a few centimetres high, whereas in their second they shoot up rapidly in late spring, forming huge, upright candelabras of flower heads up to 2m (8ft) tall. Long, elegant, bracts surround spiny flower heads that start green in summer and fade through gold to brown and almost black by winter's end. They look particularly magnificent in winter frost.

The flowers themselves are green in bud, blushing pink as they prepare to open, before turning a bluish purple. As befits such a quirky plant, they open in a strange way: starting in a horizontal central band and then progressing to either end of the flower head, rather like lighting a sparkler in the middle. Each flower head contains several thousand individual flowers, which helps explain why teasels have such a good reputation as wildlife plants. It's not only bees that adore them: when the seeds ripen they're loved by birds, especially goldfinches. Try planting some in your garden as a homegrown alternative food source to replace shop-bought nyjer seed.

The name teasel comes from the plant's historical use in cloth-making. The seed heads are perfect for gently aligning the fibres of wool (teasing) – a process known as "fulling", which makes the cloth softer and warmer. Their abilities to do this are so good they're still used by some high-end manufacturers and artisans – for mohair garments, for example, and to make the baize fabric used on billiard and card tables.

Teasel heads with curved bracts are the ones used for cloth-making. There has long been some botanical confusion as to whether there are two species or one is a variety of the other. *Dipsacus sativus* is the Fuller's teasel with downward-facing curved spikes; confusingly, *Dipsacus fullonum* is the wild teasel with straight spikes, making it much less useful.

Straight or curved, teasels are beloved of artists, printmakers, crafters and generations of children who've made "hedgehogs" by sticking eyes to the dried flower heads. Luckily, they are straightforward to grow, coping with a range of conditions but doing best in damp soil and a sunny site. They're part of the honeysuckle family, *Caprifoliaceae*, and are related to the wildflower scabious and the fashionable garden plant *Knautia macedonica*.

{PREVIOUS PAGES} Bold and unique, teasels can be useful garden plants
{OPPOSITE} Teasels' purple flowers open in an unusual pattern

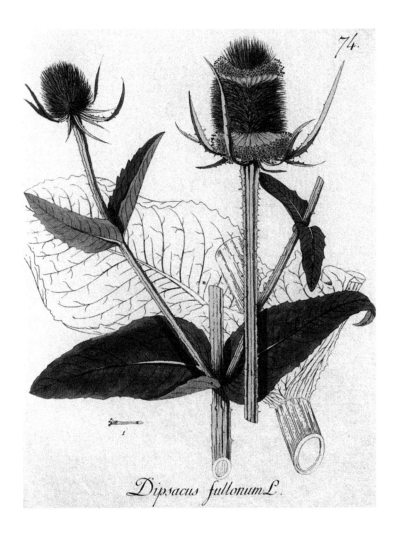

74.

Dipsacus fullonum L.

1

15

Elymus repens

Couch grass, twitch, squitch grass, scutch, quackgrass

Type of weed:	Perennial
Family:	*Poaceae*
Uses:	Edible, medicinal
Poisonous:	No

Couch grass is a difficult weed to love. It simply delights in foiling the gardener's best laid plans and it's not even pretty. Get to know it, however, and you'll find it has some surprising uses.

{LEFT} Couch's wiry, tough roots make it hard to dig up

{OPPOSITE} Historically, in times of famine the edible roots and seeds of couch grass were eaten

Pronounced "cooch", this is a tallish grass growing to about 1m (3ft) high with long, thin, grey-green blades, bearing slim seed heads with two rows of seeds along the stem. Its true horror lies below ground, where it makes a huge tangle of roots, forming dense mats that crowd out other plants. The roots are impressively strong; the sharp-tipped rhizomes can even puncture into the root balls of other plants, and are able to regenerate from the tiniest fragments.

The tenacious and invasive nature of couch grass is mainly due to its incredible quantities of roots. It has two types: fibrous feeding roots, and thicker rhizomes which are where the plant stores its energy and how it reproduces. Starchy and slightly sweet-tasting, the rhizomes have been ground into flour and used during times of famine for centuries, often to bulk out wheat flour. They won't be turning up on posh restaurant menus anytime soon, but they'd help keep you alive in a crisis. The seeds are edible too; although these are potentially quite a healthful food, they're difficult to extract and a much less abundant source of food than the roots.

Couch roots are an effective diuretic, helping remove excess water and salt from the body; they were gathered for this purpose during the Second World War by the National Herb Committee. Traditionally they were also used to treat liver, kidney and urinary problems. Cats and dogs seek out couch grass when they want to chew on something – either for its minerals or to help them vomit to clear their stomachs, often of furballs.

Probably the best use for couch is to make an organic liquid fertilizer. The plant accumulates minerals such as silica and potassium, so if you dig it up to try and get rid of it, you might as well make use of these useful nutrients by drowning the roots in a large bucket of water for a month or two (weighed down with a brick if necessary to keep them entirely underwater). Use the resultant stinky brew diluted as a liquid fertilizer on your garden. The roots should be dead and can be added to the compost heap.

If your quest to rid your garden of couch grass leaves you frustrated, try making a whistle with the leaves. Select a nice broad leaf and hold it between both thumbs. The thumb joints should touch, leaving a space between them, with the blade of grass running through the middle. Cup your hands to your mouth, palms facing outwards, and blow hard. An excruciating yet very satisfying screech ensues. Perhaps not as gratifying as a couch-free garden, but fun anyway.

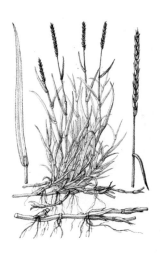

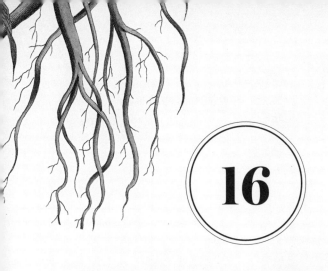

16

Epilobium or *Chamerion angustifolium*

Rosebay willowherb, fireweed, bombweed

Type of weed: Perennial	
Family: *Onagraceae*	
Uses: Edible, ornamental	
Poisonous: No	

An eruption of purple flower spikes – along with the
ripening of the first blackberries – marks a turning point
in the year. Summer has come of age, and it is rosebay
willowherb's time to shine.

Is it a weed or isn't it? Rosebay willowherb could be forgiven for being confused about whether it is welcome in gardens or not. In the past this was a relatively rare species, confined to heaths, woodland clearings, mountains and rocky screes. It was certainly well thought of: the sixteenth-century botanist John Gerard described it as "garnished with brave flowers of great beautie". According to some sources, it was cultivated as a garden plant until the 1700s.

Then came the Industrial Revolution, and suddenly the world was turned upside down. Furnaces, mines and railway lines sprouted across the land – much to the delight of rosebay willowherb, which is perfectly adapted to disturbance, rocky places and fire (hence its alternative name of fireweed).

Soon this scarce plant became much more common. The mass woodland felling caused by the First World War gave it a further boost, but it was the Second World War that really cemented rosebay's feral credentials, giving it a new name. "Fireweed" became "bombweed" as it relished the rubble-strewn, newly vacant land that bombing created. Magnificent purple spires erupted from ruined cities all over the country. After peace returned, few people were keen to grow a plant now so common and so closely associated with the suffering of wartime.

But how did rosebay willowherb manage to respond so quickly to the devastation? The key is its mobility, which comes from its incredible and slightly terrifying seeds. Each plant can produce 80,000 highly mobile seeds, each with its own beautifully fashioned parachute, ready to launch into the slightest breeze. In a scientific experiment into weed dispersal, rosebay seeds took a whole minute to reach the floor when dropped from the top of a 3m (10ft) ladder in a draught-free room. Imagine how far the wind can disperse them.

Rosebay's willow-like leaves explain its common name, but tell little of the family history. It's closely related to evening primroses (*Oenothera*), both being members of the *Onagraceae* family which includes fuchsias, gauras and clarkias. The cultivated variety *Epilobium angustifolium* 'Album' (white willowherb) is less invasive and looks striking when grown against a dark hedge. It can be seen to great effect in the famous White Garden at Sissinghurst Garden in Kent.

Borne on spikes up to 2m (6½ft) tall, the four-petalled, magenta-pink flowers contain lots of nectar and are loved by pollinating insects, especially moths. Watch the plants at dusk, and you may see colourful elephant hawkmoths visiting the flowers, or their exotic-looking caterpillars munching the foliage.

Epilobium angustifolium has a wide native distribution – growing wild in Alaska, Canada and Europe right through to Siberia. The whole plant is edible or useful; you can add flowers to salads or cook the young leaves as greens. Even the pith in the middle of the stems is edible, making an unlikely but tasty wild snack, and fireweed honey is a speciality in Alaska. Willowherb tea is much loved in Russia and other Slavic countries. It's rich in vitamin C and tannins, and is recommended by herbalists to prevent and help treat prostate cancer. With so many uses, rosebay willowherb truly is a wonderful weed.

{PREVIOUS PAGES} Rosebay willowherb is one of the prettiest "weeds" out there

{OPPOSITE} Don't be fooled by its name, rosebay willowherb is more closely related to fuchsias than willows!

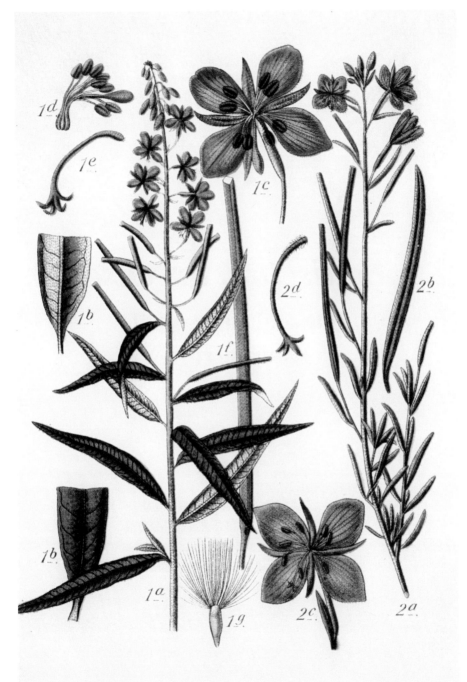

17

Equisetum arvense

Horsetail, mare's tail, scouring rush

Type of weed:	Perennial
Family:	*Equisetaceae*
Uses:	Ornamental, medicinal
Poisonous:	In large quantities

Sometimes referred to as "living fossils", horsetails are an incredibly ancient group of plants. Not just as old as the dinosaurs, they evolved millions of years *before* the dinosaurs, and long before flowering plants.

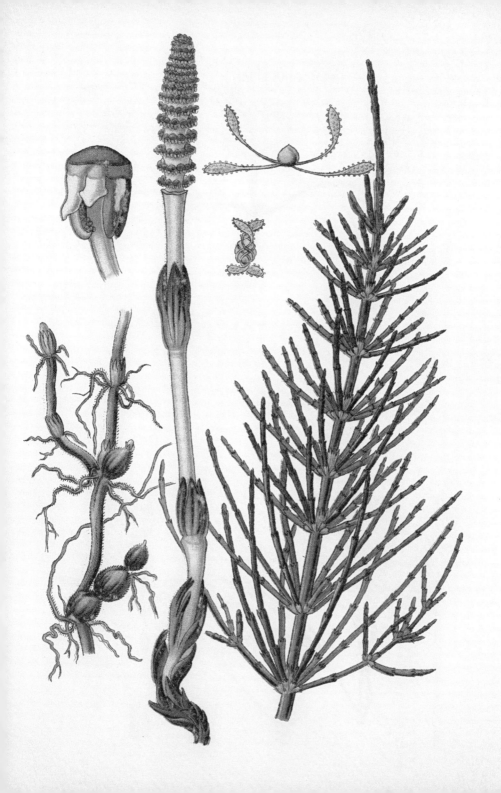

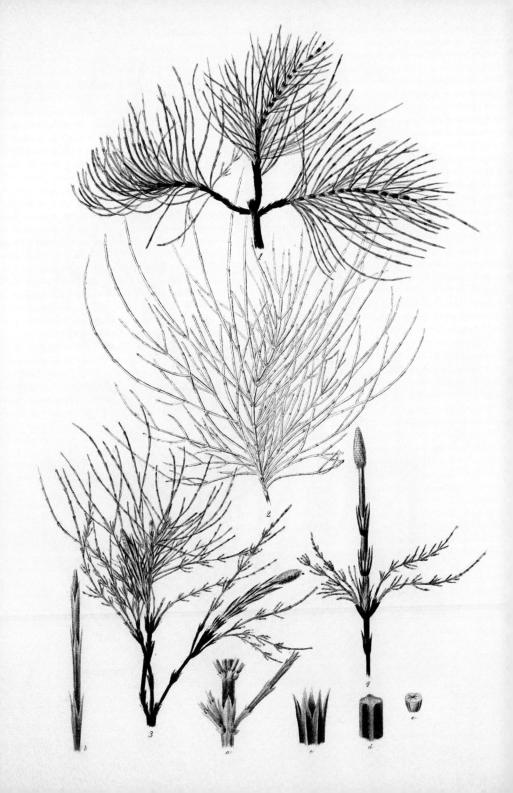

1

2

3

4

b

a

c

d

e

Theirs was a world very different to ours. During their heyday in the late Devonian and Carboniferous periods (around 380–300 million years ago), horsetail species that are now extinct grew to 20m (66ft) high and formed huge primeval forests inhabited by amazing creatures such as dragonflies with wingspans of nearly 1m (3ft) across. If you've ever picked up a lump of coal, you've touched the fossil remains of these forests – a vivid demonstration that coal really is the definitive fossil fuel!

Since those halcyon ancient times, a select few horsetails have survived asteroid impacts, seen the dinosaurs come and go, and made it to the present day. Unsurprisingly, they are very, very tough. There are several native species in Britain and Europe, the most well-known (some would say infamous) of which is *Equisetum arvense*, a common inhabitant of allotments, waste ground and gardens across the country. Its appearance is often a sign of damp, heavy soil, its stringy black roots able to go down as deep as 2m (6½ft) and its feathery, deciduous foliage growing 20–60cm (8–24in) tall.

Every part of the horsetail is peculiar. Known as pteridophytes or fern allies, they share a primitive life cycle, reproducing by spores (like fungi) rather than seeds (like flowering plants). The first sign you'll see of *Equisetum arvense* in spring is strange conelike structures called strobili, which look rather like thin toadstools. These produce the spores, and poke through the soil weeks before the leafy growth appears. The bottlebrush-like foliage is strange, too. It grows in an unusual way: each stem segment can lengthen itself independently, meaning the plant can regrow rapidly after it's damaged. As children often discover to their delight, you can pull these segments apart and put them together again, a sort of plant-based Lego.

Horsetails are able to synthesize lots of interesting chemicals, including nicotine. One of their most notable properties is that their foliage is covered in tiny silica crystals, giving it an abrasive feel. Formerly, horsetails were used for polishing metal and arrow shafts (hence the old name, scouring rush).

Modern science is beginning to unravel the importance of silica to human health, so herbal remedies like horsetail decoctions for nail, hair and bone health may yet be vindicated. However, caution is needed because the plant also contains thiaminase, which destroys vitamin B1.

The best way to control horsetail is to keep pulling it up as soon as you see it. Stew the leaves and roots in a barrel of water to capture their nutrients and make your own liquid fertilizer – or take your lead from nature and plant more. Horsetails are a striking group, and one in particular is a rather trendy garden plant. *Equisetum hyemale* has an amazing vertical form and makes regular appearances at RHS Chelsea and other flower shows. Proof that this genus, while ancient, still has a lot to offer.

{PREVIOUS PAGES} Quite unlike other plants, horsetails have a strange beauty

{OPPOSITE} The intricate structure of horsetails repays closer inspection

Ficaria verna

Lesser celandine, pilewort, fig buttercup

Type of weed: Perennial	**Uses:** Ornamental
Family: *Ranunculaceae*	**Poisonous:** Yes

Certain plants are gatekeepers of the year, full of symbolism and very much sentinels of the season. Lesser celandine is one such plant, small in stature but big in impact, its party trick being to banish the winter blues with a brazen carpet of colour.

There is a wonderful moment that happens in late February. As winter's grip begins to fade, suddenly you notice the sunlight has grown just that bit brighter. Fresh green shoots begin to appear in hedgerows and then suddenly… an explosion! Miniature suns and stars burst into bloom in gardens, woods and verges, sparkling brilliant gold. This is the celandine's time to shine.

Look closely, and you'll be able to easily recognize that lesser celandine is in the *Ranunculaceae* or buttercup family. In fact, it used to be classed as a buttercup, and is sometimes still referred to by its old name of *Ranunculus ficaria*. Its lustrous, colourful petals (strictly tepals) and simple flowers are very similar to buttercups (see page 150). Boldly coloured and reflective, buttercup petals have been shown to have unique mirror-like

qualities, reflecting ultraviolet light to attract pollinating insects. Imagine that: those shining stars are a carpet of bee beacons, glowing in colours invisible to human eyes.

Certainly, celandines are enjoyed by bees and are a useful early food source, especially for bumblebee queens emerging from hibernation. Plants can form dense colonies of heart-shaped, glossy leaves, 5–25cm (2–10in) high and with an indefinite spread. However, you can have too much of a good thing, and lesser celandine is famous for taking over shady spots in gardens. It's an invasive weed in North America, and is difficult to get rid of because the waxy leaves readily shed weedkiller, and its tiny bulbils and tubers mean it's easily spread around either by human disturbance or by natural events such as floods.

Luckily, celandines have the redeeming quality of disappearing for half the year. They'll provide a touch of greenery over winter, flower in early spring and then vanish for summer and autumn. Many gardeners don't see them as weeds at all. The famous gardener Christopher Lloyd was one of the first to appreciate not just their charm but also their habit of throwing up new varieties. He introduced 'Brazen Hussy' with lovely deep purple leaves. There are many other delightful cultivated varieties with flowers in shades of cream, yellow, orange and bronze, some with double blooms and contrasting backs to the petals, looking like miniature waterlilies.

If you're intentionally introducing lesser celandines to your garden, it really does pay to choose a cultivated variety because these tend to be prettier and less invasive. Grow them in a damp, shady spot – under deciduous trees and shrubs is ideal because you'll be able to see them in flower, then forget about them the rest of the year while the canopy closes over.

This cheery spring flower has worked its way into the hearts of gardeners and poets alike over the years. It was particularly loved by William Wordsworth (1770 to 1850), who wrote:

There is a Flower, the Lesser Celandine,
That shrinks, like many more, from cold
*   and rain;*
And, the first moment that the sun may shine,
Bright as the sun himself, 'tis out again!

{BELOW} Celandine's bright yellow flowers are a welcome sign of spring

19

Galium aparine

Cleavers, goosegrass, bedstraw, stickyweed

Type of weed:	Annual
Family:	*Rubiaceae*
Uses:	Edible, medicinal
Poisonous:	No

Goosegrass is a cunning plant. Instead of wasting
energy on growing strong woody stems, it cheats –
sprawling out over other plants to make the most
of the light. It slips, slides, scrambles and rambles,
filling the space between others, sometimes
smothering them too. But how does it do this?
It doesn't twine like bindweed, has no tendrils like
vetches, and no hooked thorns like brambles.

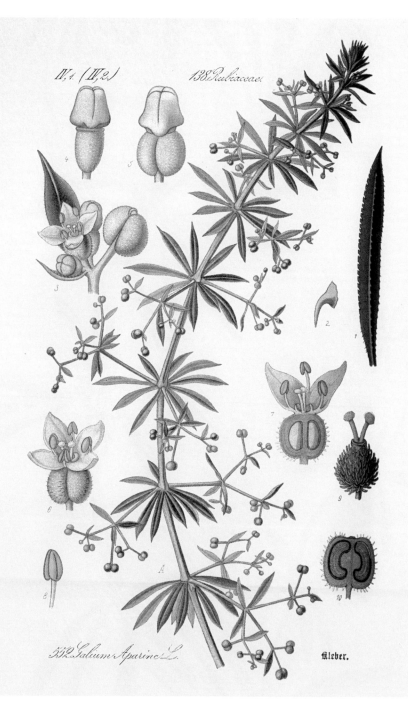

IV,1. (IV,2.)   138.Rubiaceae.

552.Galium Aparine L.   Kleber.

Goosegrass has a very clever method of climbing: trichomes. These are tiny, Velcro-like, hooked bristly hairs that help the plant grab on to others. These trichomes don't just help the plant climb, they make it stick to fur and cloth too. Hence the children's game of throwing bits of the plant at each other to stick on clothing.

Even the fruits are covered in trichomes; just like burdock fruits (see page 24), they will hitch a lift on whatever happens to be passing, be it man or beast. No wonder this plant is found almost everywhere in the world with a suitably temperate climate.

If it were bigger, we might think it looked terribly exotic. Superficially, with its ruffs of narrow leaves like the spokes of wheels, the plant looks similar to a horsetail (see page 70); however, its lax, scrambling habit and square stems are quite different. Goosegrass, strangely, is part of the coffee family (*Rubiaceae*). Look among wildflowers, and you'll see its family resemblance to other members of the same family such as lady's bedstraw (*Galium verum*) and sweet woodruff (*Galium odoratum*).

As the name suggests, goosegrass is good feed for poultry. Chickens love it. Perhaps they sense its healthy qualities: the leaves and stems are rich in minerals. It's edible for humans but not that pleasant to eat; most culinary and medicinal uses centre around infusing the plant in liquids. Young leaves can be used as greens in soups and stews, particularly in early spring when there's not much else about. Fittingly, given its family origins, the seeds can be roasted, ground and used as a coffee substitute.

The best time to harvest is early in the year, and in the "second spring" that often happens as early autumn rains and mild temperatures in September and October usher in a brief spurt of growth. Goosegrass varies hugely in size, depending on how good conditions are – it can be as small as 20cm (8in) or up to 1.5m (5ft) across.

If you don't fancy eating it or admiring its unusual structure, pull out goosegrass seedlings as soon as you see them. Plants can start setting seed very quickly. If there's already seed on the plants, wear wellies and waterproofs to pull them up, otherwise you'll get covered. Those clever little trichomes mean there's no easy way to remove the seeds apart from picking them off individually by hand. A cunning plant indeed.

{OPPOSITE} Almost every surface of *Galium aparine* is covered in bristly hairs called trichomes

20

Geranium molle

Dove's foot cranesbill, dovesfoot geranium

Type of weed:	Annual
Family:	*Geraniaceae*
Uses:	Ornamental
Poisonous:	No

This is a cute little plant, which, although it grows close to the ground, has several avian associations in its English names. "Dove's foot" comes from its deeply lobed leaves, looking like lots of feet radiating from a central point. "Cranesbill" comes from the elongated seedpods, said to look like a crane's bill. Seeing as cranes became extinct in England 400 years ago, this must be a plant with history.

Watch closely on a warm dry day, and you may be able to see why dove's foot cranesbill is such a successful weed. Those beak-shaped seed heads are, in fact, under tension – when they're fully ripe they shatter, catapulting seeds over a wide area.

Like many weeds, it's very adaptable, slotting itself in wherever it can. A lax grower, 5–30cm (2–12in) in height, dove's foot cranesbill can miniaturize itself to avoid mower blades when it grows in lawns. The entire plant is softly hairy with mid-green leaves that are roughly circular in outline and deeply lobed. Pretty little pinkish-purple flowers appear in spring and summer, sometimes into early autumn. There may be several generations a year: some plants germinate in autumn, grow slowly through winter and flower in spring; others germinate in spring and flower in summer.

The presence of dove's foot cranesbill is often a sign of dry, undernourished soil and it frequently invades lawns where the grass isn't growing strongly. This is nature's way of telling you that you need either to up your lawn maintenance regime significantly (which means a lot of work) or to stop fighting a losing battle and extend your borders so you can grow plants that enjoy the conditions more than grass does. Many wonderful plants will thrive in dry shade and look a lot happier than a threadbare lawn.

There are many cranesbills besides dove's foot. Often referred to as hardy geraniums, they are a really useful group of garden plants. They're tough and long-flowering and most grow well in sun or shade. Try 'Rozanne' or 'Orion' for months of beautiful purple-blue flowers.

Several other geranium species are weeds (see also herb robert, page 84).

Should you wish to get rid of this pretty little plant, it's easy enough to pull out from borders. If it invades your lawn, try raking the lawn before mowing to lift it up and help ensure it gets cut. Avoid putting the clippings on the compost heap if you can, because you may well just help spread it further. Feed and water to get the grass growing strongly. And finally, don't cut the grass too short – if the mower blades scalp the turf and leave bare patches of soil, it's open season for dove's foot cranesbill. But why would you want to rid yourself of such a pretty little thing?

{ABOVE AND OPPOSITE} *Geranium molle* is a close relative of the hardy cranesbills grown in gardens

21

Geranium robertianum

Herb robert, stinking bob

Type of weed:	Annual, occasionally biennial
Family:	*Geraniaceae*
Uses:	Medicinal, ornamental
Poisonous:	No

The phrase "familiarity breeds contempt" never rang truer.
Seeing the plant out of context makes it hard to imagine ever
calling this a weed – herb robert is such a delicate, pretty
little thing. If it were rare and exotic or hard to grow, we'd
undoubtedly treasure it.

For many weeks from late spring to early autumn, *Geranium robertianum* blooms brightly, throwing out dozens of vivid pink flowers. Such a bold colour could easily be jarring, yet somehow herb robert remains demure. Perhaps it's the flowers' small size, their pale pattern of veins, or their placement, sprinkled like stars on mounds of ferny foliage. Together with the reddish, wine-tinted leaves, stems and seed heads, they make a very attractive picture.

Looking to the Latin name can often be really handy for gardeners to get to know their plants. Herb robert is a *Geranium* or hardy cranesbill, related to other five-petalled beauties such as meadow cranesbill, *Geranium pratense*. It has hundreds of common names, though very few relate to cranesbills (so called because it shares the family trait of pointed seed heads like the long, sharp beaks of cranes and storks).

The most common name is "stinking bob", which comes from the plant's peculiar scent when crushed. Fragrance can be an emotive topic – while some of us don't particularly mind stinking bob's particular pong, others find it downright offensive. Luckily this scent is released only when the plant is crushed, which is yet another reason not to weed it out!

Herb robert is a lax, rambling annual (sometimes biennial, growing only leaves one year and flowering the next). Reaching between

10 and 45cm (4–18in) tall, it grows wild in woods, hedgerows and rocky places, while in gardens it tends to seed around in shady spots, sometimes forming extensive colonies.

If you try making a gravel garden somewhere a bit too shady, you're practically inviting it in. But why fight something so carefree and so beautiful? It makes a useful plant for dry shady spots, contrasting beautifully with many other plants, for example wood rushes (*Luzula*), sedges (*Carex*) and bolder plants such as hostas and purple-leaved heucheras.

White-flowered varieties exist too, such as *Geranium robertianum* 'Album' and 'Celtic White' which entirely lacks red pigment, giving the plants a fresh green appearance. 'Celtic White' is also claimed to be more compact and less prone to inviting itself all over the garden. Fortunately, controlling these plants isn't hard, as they're very easily pulled up. Alternatively hoe off seedlings or dig the plants into the soil – unlike perennial weeds, they can't regenerate from root fragments.

Highly regarded by herbalists, herb robert has many uses. The leaves have styptic properties, making them useful for stemming bleeding from minor wounds – handy if you're caught out in the garden. Traditionally they were used for nosebleeds and toothache too. Beautiful and useful, herb robert deserves a place in every garden.

{OPPOSITE} The plant's beak-like seedpods show its relation to hardy cranesbills

{ABOVE} With its vivid colouring and delicate leaves, this is a weed that's easy to love

22

Geum urbanum

Herb bennet, wood avens

Type of weed:	Perennial
Family:	*Rosaceae*
Uses:	Edible, medicinal
Poisonous:	No

Herb bennet is one of those weeds that many gardeners recognize but few can name. This is a shame, as both the English and the Latin names tell a story and help you appreciate the unusual qualities of this characterful shade-lover.

Historically this plant was also known as "clove root". Unlike many old English names, this one has a ring of truth to it: its roots do in fact have a strong, clovelike aroma and can be used as one of our very few native spices. The fragrance comes mainly from the presence of an aromatic substance called eugenol, which is also found in cloves and nutmeg. Herb bennet's roots were used to flavour beer or chewed for bad breath, and were also used as a moth repellent and in various medicinal preparations, for everything from diarrhoea to heart disease and halitosis.

While more effective medicines have now put herb bennet's medicinal properties on the back burner, you can still use the roots in cooking. Dry them and use in the same way as cloves – include the finer roots too, but use slightly increased quantities because they're not as strong. They'll add an interesting flavour to mulled wine or sweet desserts, for example.

Back in the days when people regularly looked to plants for all sorts of meanings, wood avens became associated with Christianity; the leaves growing in threes and its five-petalled flowers were considered to recall the Holy Trinity and the five wounds of Christ respectively. This led to the Latin moniker *herba benedicta*, which over time became contracted and anglicized to herb bennet.

Those five petals are typical of its kin in the *Rosaceae* or rose family, which also includes brambles, strawberries and apple trees. Looking at the Latin name, you realize this common weed is actually a cousin of some common garden plants. Geums have been cottage garden favourites for years. Their pretty flowers come in shades of yellow, orange and red, and have an airy, elegant look. The closely related water avens (*Geum rivale*) is a pretty native wildflower with rather chic, dusky pink, nodding flowers. It works well in both traditional cottage gardens and more contemporary schemes.

Like many weeds, herb bennet has some clever adaptations. Its nondescript leaves (vaguely like strawberry leaves) blend seamlessly with other plants, never drawing attention to themselves. And those scented roots are really tough, making plants physically difficult pull up by hand. It grows to around 45cm (18in) tall and bears small, lemon-yellow flowers in summer. These are followed by clusters of dry fruits known as achenes, which will be familiar to anyone with a dog or long-haired cat. The seeds have small hooks and readily attach themselves to fur and clothing to hitch a free ride to pastures new.

{LEFT} Herb bennet is a common weed in shady gardens

{OPPOSITE} The tough roots of *Geum urbanum* have a delicious scent

23

Hedera helix

Ivy, English ivy, common ivy

Type of weed:	Perennial climber
Family:	*Araliaceae*
Uses:	Ornamental
Poisonous:	Yes

When you look at what ivy is, what it can do and how much life it supports, calling it a weed seems hugely ungrateful. Aside from its amazing wildlife credentials, it's one of our most useful and versatile plants – is there another species capable of being grown as a groundcover plant, a shrub, a bedding plant, a houseplant *and* a climber?

The only evergreen climber native to Britain, ivy is a woody vine that can grow up to 30m (100ft) tall. This vigour is what scares people, but is also a part of what makes it so useful. Stand by an ivy-covered tree on a sunny October day and you'll hear it roaring with life. Its autumn flowers are hugely important for bees, butterflies and all manner of insects who will be busy making use of the countryside's last burst of pollen and nectar before winter sets in.

Ivy transforms bare tree trunks into tower blocks for wildlife. Its dense evergreen growth provides a safe and sheltered space for a myriad of life, from nesting birds to all manner of invertebrate species. The flowers are followed by berries, which provide yet more food for wildlife. More than 100 species of insects and 17 species of birds feed on ivy in the UK. There's even a special ivy bee, which looks like a fluffy ginger honeybee.

Humans benefit from ivy, too. A NASA study showed that ivy has impressive abilities to remove harmful chemicals from the air on board its spacecraft. Today it's even marketed and sold as an air-purifying houseplant. Ivy is even an effective insulator: if you grow it on the outside walls of your house, it will keep you warmer in winter and cooler in summer.

However, not all ivy climbs. Once the plant has established itself on a wall or tree it suddenly changes its habit. The plant switches from a juvenile (climbing) growth phase to an adult, shrubby (arborescent) one. Even the leaf shape changes, from five pointed to oval.

Only once it has become arborescent will it begin to produce those wildlife-tastic flowers. Interestingly, cuttings of arborescent ivy stay arborescent when planted in the ground, growing forever as shrubs.

Many people think that ivy is a parasite on trees, but this isn't true. It doesn't penetrate the bark, and has a very clever method of attachment. Ivy sticks on with green adventitious roots which initially glue themselves to whatever surface they're climbing on. They then dry out, turning brown and shrinking in the process, pulling the plant closer to its support. The only time ivy damages trees is when it makes weak, old trees top-heavy and they blow down in storms. And contrary to common belief, ivy doesn't harm sound brickwork either. However, the berries are poisonous to humans, and handling the plant can cause contact dermatitis, so wear long sleeves and gloves when you prune it.

Still, ivy is a useful garden plant, particularly for dry, shady spots and covering eyesores (not to mention bringing in the wildlife). To brighten things up choose a variegated or golden-leaf cultivar like 'Buttercup'. There are more than 100 different varieties for sale, large and small and in a range of colours, so there's bound to be one that's right for your garden.

{OPPOSITE} Ivy plants change their leaf shape and growth habit as they mature, starting as a climber but becoming shrubby after a decade or so

24

Heracleum

Heracleum sphondylium (hogweed), *H. mantegazzianum* (giant hogweed)

Type of weed:	Biennial or short-lived perennial
Family:	*Apiaceae*
Uses:	Edible, ornamental
Poisonous:	Partially

Stately and architectural, hogweeds would be strong
contenders in a weed beauty pageant. In full bloom they are
remarkable, their large, white flower heads thrumming with
pollinating insects. In death they are beautiful too, their
sculptural skeletons adorning the countryside for months on
end. Their beauty hides some surprising secrets.

Hogweed (*Heracleum sphondylium*) is a lovely plant, decorating hedgerows, grassy verges and meadows with its distinctive flat-topped flowers for months on end. The flowers are white, sometimes pink-tinged, and make perfect landing pads for insects who come to feast on their abundant nectar. Properly known as umbels, these flower heads radiate out from a central point, like an umbrella – hence the old family name *Umbelliferae*, and their English name umbellifers. Hairy stems and leaves help distinguish it from other umbellifers (now called *Apiaceae* and often referred to as the carrot family). Hogweed grows to around 1.8m (6ft) tall and is one of northwestern Europe's most striking wildflowers.

So it's no surprise that gardeners got excited when an even more dramatic version – giant hogweed, *Heracleum mantegazzianum* – was introduced from Russia in the nineteenth century. Giant hogweed is a truly stunning plant, growing up to 4m (13ft) tall with huge heads of flowers the size of bicycle wheels. Thought to be the biggest herbaceous (non-woody) plant that grows in a temperate climate, giant hogweed can also be distinguished by its more jagged leaves and purple blotches on the stem.

However, this beautiful giant has a sting in the tail. Particularly the sap, which causes dermatitis and photosensitivity, leading to serious blisters if you get it on your skin and expose to sunlight. Its seeding potential is also much increased, as each plant produces tens of thousands of seeds that are easily washed downstream in the plant's favoured riverside locations. Along with Himalayan balsam, giant hogweed is a true outlaw, being listed on the Wildlife and Countryside Act as an invasive non-native plant; and specifically mentioned in the Invasive Alien Species (Enforcement and Permitting) Order 2019. Don't grow giant hogweed in your garden and don't spread it in the wild. If you see it on a walk, just admire it from a safe distance.

If you like the look but want something less invasive, there are dozens of wonderful relatives. Giant hog fennel, *Peucedanum verticillare*, and giant fennel, *Ferula communis*, have a similar architectural effect and are rather fashionable plants among trendy garden designers. And of course, our native hogweed can be grown in gardens if you don't mind its propensity to self-seed. Just be aware that its sap can cause similar symptoms (though not as severe as giant hogweed) if you get it on your skin.

Our native hogweed has some surprising edible uses. The young leaf shoots are widely regarded as one of the best wild foraged foods, cooked like asparagus in springtime. However, a note of extreme caution is necessary, as there are plenty of similar-looking plants that are toxic. The *Apiaceae* or carrot family is home to an array of plants ranging across the spectrum from deadly to delicious; from hemlock and fool's parsley to carrots, parsnips, and coriander. Never eat a foraged food unless you're absolutely certain of its identity.

If you can be certain of the identity, native hogweed has edible seeds too, which have a lovely spicy flavour somewhere between ginger, cardamom and coriander. Best picked before they ripen fully, they work well in sweet recipes such as flapjacks or parkin, or in tea – homegrown chai, anyone?

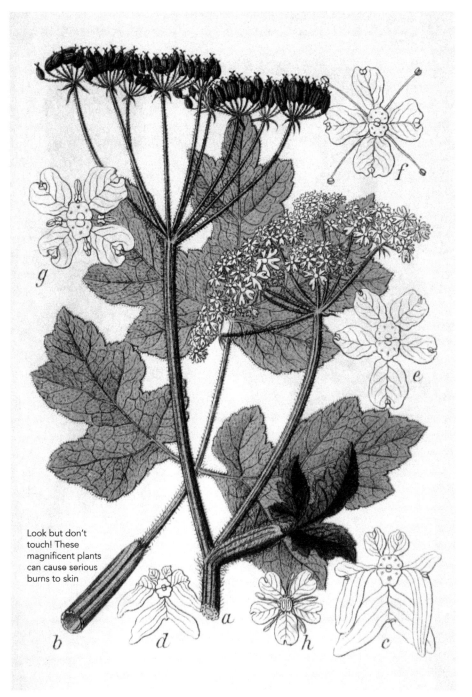

Look but don't touch! These magnificent plants can cause serious burns to skin

25

Hyacinthoides

Hyacinthoides hispanica (Spanish bluebell), *H.* × *massartiana* (hybrid bluebell), *H. non-scripta* (English bluebell)

Type of weed: Bulb	
Family: *Asparagaceae*	
Uses: Ornamental	
Poisonous: No	

Just after Christmas, vivid green shoots
begin to thrust forth from the cold soil in woodlands,
along hedge banks and in shady spots in the garden.
It's small but powerful affirmation that spring is on
its way. Slowly they expand, unfazed by frost or rain
or snow, until suddenly a flood of blue flowers
inundates the woodland floor.

A bluebell wood in full flower is a breathtaking sight – and one that's pretty much unique to Britain and Ireland; these small islands are reputed to be home to an incredible 50% of the world's bluebells. Carpets of scented blue flowers might not sound like a weed, but bluebells are very good at seeding around and bulking themselves up with new bulbs. They can form dense mats that elbow aside more delicate flowers. And among their masses, interlopers lurk...

Spanish bluebells (*Hyacinthoides hispanica*) tend to get on rather well with English bluebells, producing vigorous hybrid swarms, known in Latin as *Hyacinthoides × massartiana*. These hybrids lack the scent and distinctive deep blue colouring of English bluebells. Pollen is another way to tell them apart; *H. non-scripta* has creamy-white pollen, whereas Spanish and hybrid flowers tend to have blue or green pollen. The most sure-fire way to spot an English bluebell is by its curved, nodding head with flowers on one side only.

In Britain, Spanish and hybrid bluebells unleash all kinds of horticultural xenophobia on account of their foreignness. It's true that there's a lot to be said for the delicate charms of the native species, but if climate change threatens bluebell woods – as is predicted by some experts – perhaps the hybrids' vigour and Spanish blood may help, coming as it does from a warmer climate?

If you decide to try and control bluebells in your garden, slow and steady wins the race. You might as well enjoy the flowers; the best way is to pull up as much as you can the moment the flowers have faded. The stems will all snap, and you'll have lots of material for the compost heap. Do this for a few years running, and the plants will decline in vigour and fade away.

Unless your property borders onto a wild area with native bluebells, don't fret over the presence of Spanish or hybrid bluebells in your garden. They're unlikely to do any harm and can provide a useful source of nectar for pollinating insects. We have no chance of ever eradicating them, so we might as well learn to appreciate them. That said, we should look after our natives by always disposing of hybrid and Spanish bluebells properly when they've been dug up – municipal composting schemes are fine because they get hot enough to kill seeds and bulbs.

As author and broadcaster Richard Mabey points out, bluebells perfectly demonstrate the "weed is a plant in the wrong place" principle. While Spanish bluebells are weeds outside the garden, English bluebells are often weeds inside the garden. In an age where gardens are becoming wilder and the countryside ever more fragmented, and nature is on the march due to climate change, perhaps we should just learn to treasure the wild plants that thrive in the new conditions we have made – wherever they originally came from.

{OPPOSITE} Bluebells are much loved for spring colour in woodlands, although they can be invasive in gardens

26

Impatiens glandulifera

Himalayan balsam, Indian balsam, policeman's helmet, bee bums, jewelweed, touch-me-not

Type of weed: Annual	
Family: *Balsaminaceae*	
Uses: Edible, medicinal, ornamental	
Poisonous: No	

Taken out of context, Himalayan balsam sounds exotic and lovely, like an ingredient for posh shampoos or perfumes. So look past its "weed" label and admire it for a minute – "exotic" and "lovely" are indeed two words that come to mind.

Growing 2–3m (6–10ft) high in just one season, Himalayan balsam is a statuesque and elegant plant. Sprays of colourful hooded flowers in shades from pure white to dark pinkish-purple erupt from the leaf joints on strong upright stems. This is our tallest wild annual plant. It is showy and rather tropical-looking and has the fascinating habit of having exploding seed pods too, firing seeds up to 6m (20ft) away.

Unfortunately, those exploding seedpods get *Impatiens glandulifera* into trouble: it has colonized countless miles of riverbanks, canal sides and other damp places. Although some scientists are beginning to think its impact is not as bad as was first thought, Himalayan balsam is now on two official wanted lists: the UK's Schedule 9 of the Wildlife and Countryside Act, and the Invasive Alien Species (Enforcement and Permitting) Order 2019. To put it simply: do not grow this plant in your garden or help it spread in the wild. If you like the look and fancy growing something similar (but not illegal) in your garden, try the perennial *Impatiens tinctoria*, which has gorgeously lily-scented, pure white flowers with a red stain in the centre. Busy lizzies, the popular bedding plants, are close relatives too.

As the plant's name suggests, Himalayan balsam is native to the western flank of the Himalayas, a habitat at high altitude (even the lowest part of its range is more than 1.6 km/1 mile above sea level), which explains its hardiness to cool British summers. It's a favourite of bees – hence one of its common names, "bee bums". If you pass a patch of it in full flower on a sunny day, a lot of bee bums

is what you'll see. The flowers are incredibly nectar-rich, and balsam honey is fragrant, light-coloured and runny. Balsam's late flowering is useful to bees and helps bridge the gap in the nectar flow between the blooming of early summer flowers and ivy in autumn.

Strange, whitish "ghost bees" are occasionally reported to the British Beekeepers Association. They're simply covered in the pale pollen of Himalayan balsam, which has a sophisticated way of ensuring it is able to reproduce. The flowers systematically brush pollen over the backs of visiting bees: as they enter the flower, they set off a trigger that makes the stamen descend to deposit pollen on the bee.

Humans can make use of balsam, too. The seeds are edible either ripe or unripe (unripe are tastier and are easier to harvest because the seedpods won't explode on you). They have a nutty flavour and can be eaten in sweet or savoury dishes, added to a crumble topping, sprinkled over curries or thrown over a salad*.

A true vegetable vagabond, Himalayan balsam is a bold and beautiful plant that turns some of our most polluted industrial backwaters into a sea of flowers. Adored by bees yet outlawed by humans, this plant shows the fascinating interplay between botany and humanity. Its story is still unfolding.

*Be aware that it's illegal to transport the plant (except for eradication purposes), so these uses are mentioned for interest only.

{PREVIOUS PAGES AND OPPOSITE} Himalayan balsam's flowers vary between white and deep purple; there are several closely related species with yellow flowers

27

Jacobaea vulgaris, aka *Senecio jacobaea*

Ragwort, common ragwort, mare's fart, tansy ragwort

Type of weed: Biennial

Family: *Asteraceae*

Uses: Ornamental

Poisonous: Yes

As summer hits its stride, schools empty and beaches
fill up with holidaymakers, clusters of golden stars begin
to dot the countryside. On abandoned land, grassy verges
and allotments, these stars shine bright, sometimes
coalescing into a shimmering tapestry of golden yellow.
This is ragwort's moment.

The renowned countryside poet John Clare wrote of ragwort in the 1830s:

What time the summer binds her russet sheaves;
Decking rude spots with beauties manifold
That without thee were dreary to behold,
Sunburnt and bare —

Hundreds of species of bees, butterflies and pollinating insects flock to these open, nectar-rich flowers. Dozens of native invertebrate species feed on nothing else. One of our most colourful moths, the bright red and black cinnabar moth (*Tyria jacobaeae*), feeds too, although it has other things on its mind. It

lays eggs, hundreds of them. Soon, swarms of caterpillars, orange and black like some strange kind of liquorice allsort, begin to devour the plants. It's a colourful spectacle and one that's been going on for many thousands of years.

Yet these days, ragwort is a true vagabond. There is even specific legislation (the Ragwort Control Act, 2003) aimed at curbing its spread. Why would an indigenous and undeniably wildlife-friendly plant be so demonized?

It pays to look again at those caterpillars. They're very brightly coloured, and those dramatic orange and brown stripes serve as a warning: *Don't eat me, or you'll regret it.* Highly toxic, they get their poison from their diet. Ragwort is full of toxic alkaloids, and this is what gets it into trouble.

If grazing animals, especially horses, eat ragwort, they can get liver failure and die. This sounds dramatic, but it's important to note that ragwort is unpalatable (the crushed foliage smells awful – hence the old common name "mare's fart") and horses tend to avoid it if they can.

Unfortunately, there are several ways humans short-circuit ragwort's attempts to avoid being eaten. When it's mixed in with dried hay or fermented silage, it's much harder for animals to avoid. And so too, ironically, when it's out in the field, withered and dying from weedkiller. The other danger comes when animals don't have enough space or food and pastures become overgrazed, and hungry mouths alight on ragwort from sheer desperation. All these are human influences conspiring to make problems between plants and animals that have for the most part lived together for thousands upon thousands of years.

So what is the gardener to do? If your garden is within 50m (55 yards) of land used for grazing, or for hay or silage production, you should remove ragwort growing on your land*. Always wear gloves and long sleeves when handling the plant. Yellow yarrows such as *Achillea* 'Moonshine' make an attractive, wildlife friendly and non-toxic alternative in high risk areas.

If you're nowhere near land used for grazing or forage production, you're fine to enjoy ragwort's bright flowers and appreciate the wildlife it brings in. The government guidance on the legislation itself admits: "Ragwort... is very important for wildlife ... It supports a wide variety of invertebrates and is a major nectar source for many insects." Even vagabonds have their place.

*For more information see the *Code of Practice on How to Prevent the Spread of Ragwort* from Defra, which, is available online.

{OPPOSITE} Ragwort is a wildlife magnet

{LEFT} The daisy-like flowers show this plant's place in the *Asteraceae* or daisy family

28

Lamium

Lamium purpureum (red deadnettle), *Lamium album* (white deadnettle)

Type of weed: Perennials and annuals	
Family: *Lamiaceae*	
Uses: Edible, medicinal, ornamental	
Poisonous: No	

"Deadnettles" is a rather horrible name for a rather lovely group of plants. Unrelated to true nettles, they have no sting (hence the name, deadnettle). Their square stems are a giveaway as to their true identity as part of the mint family (*Lamiaceae*). If you look closely, you'll see their pretty, hooded flowers are rather like those of their relatives, salvias and rosemary.

Red deadnettle, *Lamium purpureum*, is a "winter weed" in many areas, its wine-tinged growth hiding away in the winter murk, ready for that sunny weekend when suddenly you realize that spring has sprung. The first daffodils are out, the light is bright and clear, and all at once your allotment is covered in pretty little plants sticking their pinky purple tongue-like flowers out at you. In sunny sites, the purple tint of the leaves is an attractive feature in its own right. Height varies with site and conditions: 5cm (2in) in exposed sunny allotments or fields, up to 45cm (18in) in lush hedgerows.

Those bright little tongues – such a lovely colour when they occur in beds and borders against the yellow crocuses, daffodils and grape hyacinths – are great for bees. They're a lifeline for bumblebees emerging from hibernation, and are a particular favourite of our furry, ginger-blonde, common carder bees. The flowers look like tongues from above but open mouths when you get close, and the fuzzy leaves have a purple colour that always gets deeper towards the plant's tips. Red deadnettle is an annual plant that can have several generations a year. Summer plants are larger, looser and less frequent.

There are several other species that you may encounter in gardens. The most common is the white deadnettle, *Lamium album*, which is the most realistic nettle mimic of all. A bee-friendly perennial plant reaching 20–60cm (8–24in) high, it often grows right alongside real nettles in shady sites. Although the leaves are very similar, you can spot the fake a mile off by its pretty creamy-white whorls of flowers – real nettles have strange catkin-like tassels instead. With its long flowering season from late spring right through to winter, this is one weed that's worth keeping.

The spotted deadnettle, *Lamium maculatum*, has bright silvery leaves and vivid flowers; there are many garden-worthy cultivars such as 'Beacon Silver', which has lovely magenta flowers, smart leaves and grows well in dry shade.

Deadnettles are edible: young shoots can be used in salads or more mature growth can be cooked as a pot herb (added to soups, stews, pasta dishes and the like). However, the best bit by far is the flowers of the white deadnettle; use them as a garnish for desserts or pluck them straight from the plant to suck out their sweet nectar (like an off-season honeysuckle).

{OPPOSITE} White deadnettle's flowers are great for bees and last well in a vase, too

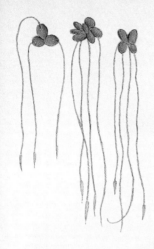

29

Lemna minor
Common duckweed

Type of weed:	Aquatic plant
Family:	*Araceae*
Uses:	Edible
Poisonous:	No

Duckweed might seem familiar, but look closely:
every single thing about it is strange and incredible.
One of the world's smallest flowering plants, it can
make water look like land, and it's even edible.

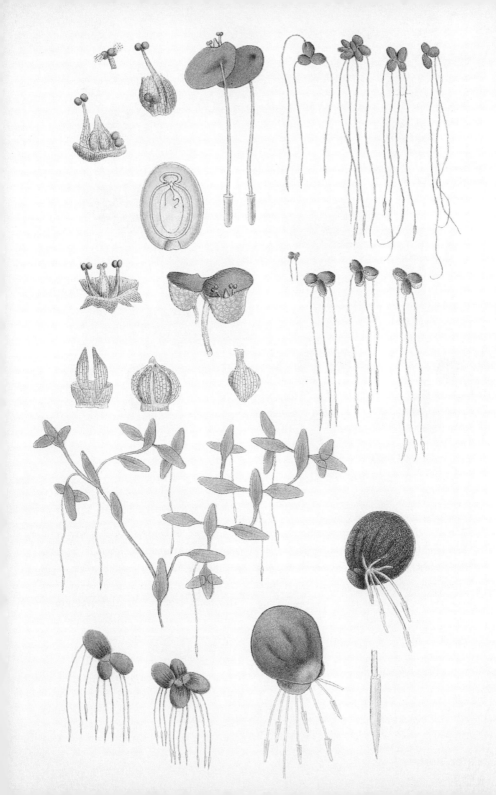

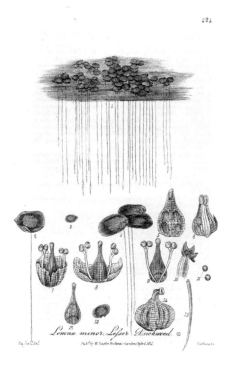

Lemna minor. Lesser Duckweed.

Looking at duckweed's tiny oval floating pads, each with a single root that dangles into the water, you'd never believe it's related to the Swiss cheese plant (*Monstera deliciosa*). They're both members of the arum family, *Araceae*, along with another common houseplant, the peace lily (*Spathiphyllum*).

However, although it can flower and set seed like most plants do, it mainly reproduces by cloning itself (by producing an identical offshoot in a process known as "budding"). This helps explain why duckweed grows so quickly and can cover a whole pond in just a few weeks. Scientists have calculated that duckweed can double its biomass in less than two days in optimal conditions; a 10-cm (4-in) square patch could (in the absence of constraints like shade or animals eating it) grow to cover a hectare (2½ acres) in under 50 days. That's from a saucer size to a rugby pitch in less than two months – a ten million-fold increase!

This vigorous growth helps to clean the water below, and can be used in a process called "phytoremediation" to remove industrial pollution and excess nutrients from farm runoff.

Duckweed is an important part of the aquatic food chain too. It shelters lots of aquatic life, which you'll often see wriggling about if you fish it out of your pond, and it even cuts down algae and mosquito larvae problems.

There are many ways you can make use of duckweed. You can put it on your compost heap, especially if you have lots of dry, woody material to mix with it. A useful permaculture plant, it makes great food for chickens and, as the name suggests, ducks. Duckweed is finding fame as a food for people too. It's high in protein and has rebranded as "water lentil" by canny manufacturers, and is also used powdered as a protein supplement. However, the plant contains calcium oxalate crystals so it needs to be processed before consumption.

A clever little plant, *Lemna minor* is great at hitching lifts on migratory birds and is found almost everywhere in the world apart from deserts and polar regions. Duckweed grows in still or slow-flowing water and often makes still pools look like lush lawns. However, it can also grow on land; on mud and damp rocks or stonework. Weirdly, it shares a habit with drought-loving cacti in that it doesn't even differentiate between stems and leaves. It just is.

The quirkiness doesn't stop there. Duckweed has a strange lifecycle: as the temperature falls in autumn, it produces carbohydrate-rich buds known as turions, which sink to the bottom of the pond to overwinter. As the water warms up in spring, each turion expels a gas bubble and floats back to the surface so the plant can continue growing. Useful, unusual and pretty much unstoppable, this plant's incredible powers should earn it at least a little respect from us.

{OPPOSITE} Tiny yet mighty, duckweeds have amazing reproductive powers

{PREVIOUS PAGES} Duckweeds and their relatives *Wolffia* are some of the world's smallest flowering plants

30

Malva sylvestris
Common mallow

Type of weed:	Perennial
Family:	*Malvaceae*
Uses:	Edible, medicinal, ornamental
Poisonous:	No

Being not only edible but medicinal and ornamental too, mallow is one of the friendliest wild plants. If it were hard to grow, we'd all be buying it. But because it has the temerity to grow so freely, uninvited, in such undignified spots as pavement cracks, it is tarred forever with the label "weed".

Common mallow is, as its name suggests, a common plant. Frequently found in dry spots including pavements, waste ground, verges, allotments and hedges, it grows between 30 and 120cm tall (1–4ft), making lush, leafy clumps.

Blooming for months on end over the summer, mallow has amazing flower power. Look closely in summer, and you'll see tightly packed bunch of buds at the top of each stem, and more clusters of buds where each leaf joins the stem – it just doesn't stop. Its pretty five-petalled blooms are pink with dark purple stripes, and are loved by painted lady butterflies and all manner of bees.

The palmate (hand-shaped) leaves have five lobes and prettily scalloped edges. Mallow has long been used as both food and medicine. The roots have mucilaginous properties, making them useful for poultices to treat minor burns and fresh wounds, while preparations made from the leaves can be used to treat chapped or dry skin. Probably the easiest way to make use of their medicinal properties is to add a handful of leaves to the bath. Alternatively, dry the flowers for a comforting tea.

Modern science has confirmed that common mallow contains powerful antioxidants, unsaturated fatty acids and many essential minerals along with several B vitamins and vitamin C. Its leaves are often used in winter soups in Mediterranean countries. The flowers are edible too, making a very attractive edible garnish for drinks and all sorts of dishes both sweet and savoury.

Unripe mallow seeds are known as "cheeses" and can be nibbled as a nice foraged snack or briefly fried. They have a slightly nutty taste and grow in neat, flattish circular capsules, looking like tiny model pumpkins encased in the remains of the flower's protective calyx.

The mallow family or *Malvaceae* is a huge family, full of pretty, quick-growing, colourful and often edible plants. Hollyhocks, hibiscus, abutilons, cocoa and even okra are cousins to common mallow. *Malva neglecta* (dwarf or roundleaf mallow) is a much lower-growing and less showy plant, a pavement specialist and definitely more deserving of the label "weed". *Malva moschata* or musk mallow is a beautiful native wildflower, one of the most garden-worthy of all. Tree mallow, *Malva arborea,* is a fun, quick-growing plant like a shrubby hollyhock on steroids that grows to 3m (10ft) tall in just two years. It's a great one to grow with kids or in a new-build garden while you're waiting for slower-growing plants to bulk out. Whether for food, for medicine, for ornamental value or just for fun, common mallow and its cousins are definitely plants worth getting to know.

{OPPOSITE} Mallow is closely related to several common garden plants such as hollyhocks

31

Matricaria discoidea

Pineapple weed, rayless mayweed

Type of weed: Annual	
Family: *Asteraceae*	
Uses: Edible, medicinal	
Poisonous: No	

A strange-looking plant with an unexpected scent, pineapple weed is a perfect example of how certain species can use mankind's habits to their advantage. Our twentieth-century love affair with cars literally drove its spread from Kew Gardens right across Britain in just a few decades.

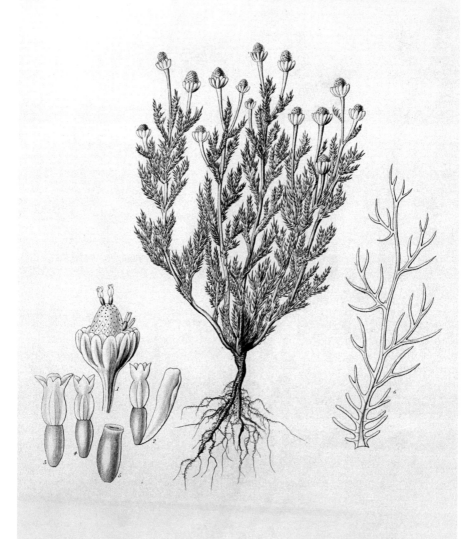

Pineapple weed looks rather like it belongs underwater – with its much-branched growth covered in tiny, rich green feathery leaves, it has a distinctively seaweedy appearance. This slightly otherworldly look is compounded by its peculiar flowers, which look like green bobbly pinecones, with a similar texture to the centre of a sunflower or chrysanthemum flower.

This is no coincidence: as a member of the *Asteraceae* or daisy family (see also daisies page 36), it has compound flowers, so what looks like one flower is in fact many tiny ones grouped together. In this case they are "ray-less" flowers, hence the alternative common name of rayless mayweed. Ray flowers are the ones on the edge of a sunflower, bearing the bright yellow petals. Disc flowers (florets) are the bobbly ones in the middle of the bloom: hence rayless mayweed has no petals. However, despite its lack of petals to advertise to pollinators, bees and hoverflies seem to enjoy visiting the flowers which are borne over a long season from May to November.

One of the twentieth century's fastest-spreading weeds, pineapple weed is thought to have first escaped from Kew Gardens in 1871, just a few years before the motor car was invented. Its timing couldn't have been better. If cars were liberating for people, they were a game changer for pineapple weed. Well adapted to be spread by the hooves and feet of animals, its tiny seeds now suddenly had a supercharged means of transport in the treads of tyres. And in the days before tarmac, there was also an ample supply of muddy, compacted and open ground

to colonize – exactly the kind of conditions *Matricaria discoidea* relishes.

Pineapple weed wasn't fazed by the coming of "metalled" roads sealed in tarmac, either. The massive expansion of the road network provided plenty more vacant, disturbed ground to colonize. Ever-increasing numbers of cars provided the perfect vehicle for *Matricaria discoidea* to conquer pretty much the whole of Britain in just a few decades. It now grows almost everywhere apart from highest, most inaccessible mountains. Growing up to 30cm (1ft) tall, it's an amazingly resilient plant: you can tread on it and it will spring back, looking exactly the same as it did before.

The plant's eponymous scent comes in part from myrcene, an aromatic compound that is also found in lemongrass, thyme and cardamom, and which is important in the fragrance industry. The flowers are the most fragrant part and are best picked young, before the seeds ripen. Medicinally it is not much used today, though historically it was used in a similar way to chamomile for its calming effects on the body, as a carminative (preventing wind) and for treating parasitic worms.

You can make an infusion of pineapple weed flowers and honey and use in ice lollies, as a cordial or in iced tea – they'll be sure to baffle anyone trying to guess what they're made from. Who knew such exotic scents were lurking at our feet?

{OPPOSITE} Despite looking almost like a delicate aquatic plant, pineapple weed is at home in hot dry places

32

Papaver cambricum aka *Meconopsis cambrica*

Welsh poppy, pani Cymraeg

Type of weed:	Perennial
Family:	*Papaveraceae*
Uses:	Ornamental
Poisonous:	Slightly

Pretty, native, colourful, shade-loving and even good for bees – yet because we didn't buy them or plant them, we weed them out. What a pity that Welsh poppies are often condemned as a weed through their sheer enthusiasm!

One of the skills that really good gardeners have is to be able to recognize all manner of seedlings, and evaluate them for what they can offer before deciding whether to weed them out. Welsh poppies willingly seed themselves into all sorts of nooks and crannies and can often be a very helpful filler in shady spots. Learning to spot potentially useful volunteers (aka "weeds") can make your garden more beautiful and much less work.

The pioneering Victorian gardener William Robinson was an early proponent of the wilder style of gardening, and he was full of praise for Welsh poppies, calling them "cheerful in all seasons" and "handsome" while also praising their fresh foliage and ability "to hold [their] own anywhere". His comment "determined colonizer" does, however, hint at their weedy potential.

Also known as *Meconopsis cambrica*, the Welsh poppy is at home in the mountains but seems to be developing a taste for life at lower altitudes. It is native from northwestern Spain through France, southwestern England and Wales. Fresh green, divided foliage makes a mound up to 30cm (1ft) high, while its flowers and seed heads can take it to 60cm (2ft) tall.

The wild type is normally yellow, with four crinkled bright yellow petals, like chiffon fabric or crepe paper, surrounding a central ring of fluffy lighter yellow stamens. Cultivated varieties include doubles, semi doubles, oranges, and 'Frances Perry' which is a rich scarlet red (keep it away from yellows, or the seedlings will lose their colouring). *Papaver cambricum* var. *aurantiacum* is a naturally occurring orange variant – its zesty flowers make quite a statement in shady spots.

Those large, open flowers bloom from May to September and are great for pollinating insects. In common with other poppies, they have lovely seedpods, like little elongated pepper pots, quite architectural-looking close up. If you've got too much of a good thing, simply snip off the flowers as they fade to control their spread. However, if you want to grow them, it pays to know that germination can be sporadic; the easiest thing to do is sprinkle seeds where you want them to grow and keep an eye out over the following 12 months.

Welsh poppies' love of rocky crevices makes them well adapted to life with humans. They frequently grow in gravel paths and cracks in walls. This habit makes them great for softening hard edges, which is particularly useful if you've got a new garden and want to get it looking established quickly. They do well in shade and look lovely with ferns and hostas, especially blue-leaved ones that will really set off the yellow-orange flowers a treat. Or grow them alongside alkanet, yellow corydalis and bluebells for a colourful blue and yellow symphony of spring weeds.

{OPPOSITE} With its delicate tissue-paper blooms, Welsh poppy is an undoubtedly beautiful "weed"

33

Pentaglottis sempervirens

Green alkanet, evergreen bugloss

Type of weed: Perennial	
Family: *Boraginaceae*	
Uses: Edible, ornamental	
Poisonous: No	

"Come and see my *Pentaglottis sempervirens*" has a rather nice ring to it, doesn't it? This is a lovely plant whose Latin name has more than a touch of Harry Potter about it. *Penta-glottis* means "five-tongues", referring to the five-petalled flowers; *semper-virens* translates as "always-living", referring to its evergreen nature.

The English name of this plant is interesting. "Alkanet" is derived from the Arabic word for henna. It's thought that alkanet was used as a dye plant; a cheaper, homegrown substitute for exotic and expensive henna.

Green alkanet is one of those cunning plants that hides in plain sight for much of the year. Its mid-green, bristly leaves (like borage and comfrey, to which it's closely related) are, to be frank, unremarkable. It grows quietly away, just getting on with it, biding its time...

Then spring arrives. Those nondescript clumps suddenly burst forth with vigorous spikes of lovely bright blue flowers up to 1m (3ft) tall. Flowering can start as early as March; it peaks in May and continues into summer. The flowers' colour is remarkable, varying in lightness slightly from plant to plant and over the weeks, but it is always a very pure sky blue that few plants can match.

Although they don't taste of much, the flowers are edible and make a very pretty decoration for cakes, desserts and salads. They're enjoyed by wildlife too, being a particular favourite of bumblebees. However, it pays to cut your plants back promptly after flowering to prevent alkanet from seeding around and taking over.

Green alkanet is a bit of a shady character, preferring to shelter in damper areas of the garden away from harsh sunlight. When conditions suit, it can be quite an aggressive spreader. Its roots are very stubborn; they go down a long way and break easily – if you want to get rid, the best option is to just keep digging.

If you love the blue flowers but perhaps want something a little less invasive, look to alkanet's relatives. Many people sense their botanical links without realizing, and wonder if alkanet is some giant variety of forget-me-not (*Myosotis*) when they first see it. It's an understandable near miss, as they are fellow members of the borage family, *Boraginaceae*. However, alkanet's flowers have a distinctive white eye and this, along with the plants' much larger size, is an easy way to tell them apart. (Forget-me-nots also have yellow centres.) Another borage family member, *Anchusa* 'Loddon Royalist' is perhaps the best blue plant you can grow, both in terms of being easy to cultivate and the depth of its flower colour. But neither anchusas nor forget-me-nots have quite the staying power of green alkanet, which will bring a sea of blue, alive with bees, that grows without a care in the world.

{OPPOSITE} Sky-blue flowers and bristly leaves belie this plant's close relation, the herb borage

Plantago major
Broadleaf plantain

| **Type of weed:** Perennial | **Uses:** Edible, medicinal, ornamental |
| **Family:** *Plantaginaceae* | **Poisonous:** No |

Don't judge a book by its cover. While broadleaf plantain is a bit of an ugly duckling, it nonetheless has many interesting properties and can be used as food, medicine and even as a garden plant.

A compacted soil specialist, this is one of those plants you can drive over and it will barely notice. Broadleaf plantain is very tolerant of trampling and is frequently found on paths, driveways, worn areas of lawns and by farmyard gates. Compaction does terrible things to soil, literally squeezing the air and life out of it – plantain is nature's rescue remedy, as its tough fibrous roots simultaneously break up compressed layers while protecting soil from future erosion. These strong roots also help the plant accumulate useful quantities of minerals such as calcium and sulphur, adding to its health-giving qualities when consumed (it is useful in pasture too for grazing animals).

When pushed, plantain will flatten itself to just a few millimetres above the soil; however, when freed from mower blades or constant trampling, it grows 10–15cm (4–6in) tall or more, with broad, mid-green leaves somewhat like miniature hostas. Each plant is a clump of oval-shaped light green leaves growing on stalks from a central rosette. Tail-like spikes of insignificant flowers (giving rise to the alternative, if rather horrid, name of rat-tail plantain) quickly ripen to tiny edible seeds.

It's not the most palatable of plants, but it has many useful properties, being rich in vitamins A, C, and K, which helps blood to clot. You can use young leaves in soups, risottos and pasta dishes for its nutritional value and mushroomy flavour. (Chew the raw plant for a few seconds; it is slightly bitter at first, then a distinctly fungal flavour fills your mouth.) Be aware, though, that excess consumption can cause a drop in blood pressure.

One of the nine sacred herbs of the Saxons (alongside mugwort, see page 28), broadleaf plantain has medicinal qualities that are still used today. The leaves have antibacterial properties and make a useful first aid remedy for minor cuts and scrapes. Crush them to release their juice and apply directly to the wound. The plant can also be used on insect bites, stings, sores, spots and rashes.

A trick for identifying plantain is to gently pull the mature leaves apart close to their base: the leaf will split, but the ribs will remain intact like pieces of string linking the severed parts of the leaf. In the United States, plantain was sometimes known as "white man's foot" because it followed Europeans closely when they headed west into the interior of the continent, creating disturbed and damaged habitats and inadvertently transporting the seeds.

Perhaps more interesting than straightforwardly beautiful, there are a number of ornamental varieties of broadleaf plantain available. *Plantago major* 'Rubrifolia' and 'Rosularis' (rose plantain)

have striking leaves the colour of red wine. The botanical oddity 'Bowles' Variety' has strange green bracts instead of flowers, making quite a talking point. Several variegated varieties are available; they could make a good substitute for small hostas if your garden has a slug problem.

{BELOW} Useful and tough, this is a common weed in dry, compacted soil

35

Prunella vulgaris

Self-heal, heal-all

Type of weed:	Perennial
Family:	*Lamiaceae*
Uses:	Edible, medicinal, ornamental
Poisonous:	No

Prunella vulgaris sounds like a great name for a botanical-themed drag queen. But is she a friend or foe? Weed or wildflower? Self-heal may not be appreciated by fans of sterile bowling green lawns, but for the rest of us there's a lot to like.

Take a closer look and her beauty becomes easily apparent. Intricately constructed, burnished coppery flower heads bear vivid purple flowers which are adored by bees. This is one of the plants that helps convince people to turn their lawns into wildflower meadows.

A spreading, prostrate perennial that enjoys moist soil, self-heal has a number of features common to the mint family (*Lamiaceae*). Its leaves grow opposite each other along square stems, and each pair of leaves is at right angles to the next. The structural flower heads, also typical of the mint family, are known as verticillasters. Flower colour can vary considerably – violet-blue, white or pink ones occasionally crop up – and plants have a long flowering period from late spring to autumn.

When given free rein, self-heal can grow as tall as 30cm (12in). But, like many weeds adapted to growing in lawns, it's adept at miniaturizing itself to escape from harm and can grow as short as 5cm (2in). The intensity of colouring and the beauty of the flower head seems to respond to environmental stimuli: when freed from the threat of lawnmower blades, the flowers are larger and have time to mature properly, and the sepal coloration is deeper; the full elegance of *Prunella vulgaris* is only revealed if she's given room to shine. It's a very good reason to leave the mower in the shed. If you like the look of self-heal but wish it were just a little bolder, try growing *Prunella grandiflora* – which, as the name suggests, is a larger-flowered form, even more showy and well suited to garden borders. It is available in shades of pink, white and purple.

The whole plant is edible; young leaves can be used in salads or as a pot herb (cooked like spinach), but its main uses have historically been medicinal, including as a poultice for skin irritation and nettle stings. The tea was used to treat sore throats, fevers, diarrhoea, liver and heart problems. Modern-day chemical analysis has confirmed the presence of ursolic acid in self-heal. Ursolic acid has been shown to have antioxidant, anti-inflammatory and anti-cancer effects.

Self-heal's star property, though, as the name suggests, comes from its use as a wound dressing: not only does it have antimicrobial properties, it also has styptic properties (stopping bleeding). For minor cuts or scrapes, macerate the leaves, stems and flowers to make a rough paste; pack this over the wound and put a plaster or gauze over it and replace regularly. Cooled self-heal tea made from the leaves and flowers can be gargled for sore throats and mouth ulcers. Some people with a more holistic view of health and

wellbeing read further into self-heal's properties in this area and consider it good for loosening the throat chakra and encouraging speaking up or speaking one's truth.

{OPPOSITE} Prunella's colourful flowers are a wildlife magnet

{ABOVE} Square stems and aromatic leaves are signs this plant is part of the mint family, Lamiaceae

36

Pseudofumaria lutea
aka *Corydalis lutea*

Yellow corydalis, yellow fumitory, rock fumewort

Type of weed:	Perennial
Family:	*Papaveraceae*
Uses:	Ornamental
Poisonous:	Toxic if consumed in large quantities

A sweet little thing, this is a plant that slips between
the cracks, in both a literal and metaphorical sense. It finds
itself at home between stones in walls and between our
definitions of "garden plant" and "weed".

A habit of turning up uninvited is the crux of the matter. People are slightly wary of it, which is a shame because yellow corydalis is very pretty and definitely worth growing as a garden plant. Look closely, and you'll see it's a close cousin of another common garden weed, fumitory (*Fumaria*). Hence its Latin name, *Pseudofumaria*. The name "fumitory" comes from an old word for smoke (also the root of our modern word "fume"), a reference to their incredibly delicate greyish foliage that can look like a haze of smoke from afar.

Yellow corydalis isn't quite so floaty-looking, but it's still delicate and pretty enough to pass as a garden plant. It makes cloudlike, ferny mounds of evergreen leaves up to 40cm (16in) in both height and spread, although when it lives in tiny cracks in walls it will grow to less than half this size. Pretty yellow flowers – clusters of sulphur yellow tubes that widen out to a flared entrance stained a deeper, egg yolk colour – adorn plants from May to August or even into autumn.

Apart from the self-seeding it is well behaved, growing healthily in shade and self-deadheading after its copious flowering. Seedlings are easy to recognize and easy to pull out. Yellow corydalis doesn't seem to suffer many pests and diseases either. Sometimes plants will suffer in extreme summer heat and drought, or in wet winters, but normally they'll have seeded around and found their spot.

Native to the southern and eastern foothills of the Alps, *Pseudofumaria lutea* has been grown in European gardens for hundreds of years. Recently it seems to be expanding its range, helped perhaps by climate change and humanity's insatiable desire to make ever more disturbed ground, buildings and walls for it to live in. Yellow corydalis particularly loves old walls, and will seed into cracks in pavements and in bare stony ground and brick rubble in abandoned sites.

A member of the *Papaveraceae* or poppy family, yellow corydalis has many relatives that make lovely garden plants. Blue-flowered corydalis are striking, and lack the yellow's profuse self-seeding habit. One of the best is the cheekily named *Corydalis* 'Tory MP' – named by its breeder for its "true blue colouring and tendency to go on a bit (flowering that is)!" Other close relatives include bleeding hearts (*Lamprocapnos*, formerly known as *Dicentra*) which are similarly colourful, intricate and soft-textured in both leaf and flower.

{RIGHT AND OPPOSITE}
It might look delicate but this plant is tough enough to grow in walls

37

Pteridium aquilinum

Bracken, brackenfern

Type of weed: Perennial	
Family: *Dennstaedtiaceae*	
Uses: Edible (controversial)	
Poisonous: Partially	

When describing bracken, it is difficult to avoid superlatives. The largest fern native to the British Isles, it's also thought to be Britain's single most common wild plant. Bracken is also one of the world's most widespread plants, growing on every continent except Antarctica.

A very ancient plant, bracken has been growing round the world for tens of millions of years. Yet it remains somewhat controversial, being particularly hated by the UK's moorland farmers for increasingly taking over pastureland. ("If it wasn't native, it would be considered a national emergency," says botanist and author Ken Thompson.) But for the vast majority of us who live in towns and cities, this feisty fern is uniquely beautiful.

Fronds up to 4m (13ft) long have been recorded, although in woodlands it normally tops out at 1.5m (5ft), while on exposed moorlands 1–1.2m (3–4ft) is more normal. Bracken is distinguishable from our other native ferns by its tall canelike growth that comes from multiple points underground (rather than a central crown), and its branched fronds that die back over winter.

From its zingy green unfurling fiddleheads (croziers) in spring, through lush canopies of verdant foliage in summer, to its yellow-orange-rust transformation in autumn, bracken is an important part of the countryside scene in many areas. Although unbroken bracken stands might seem like a lifeless monoculture, they do support some wildlife such as adders and birds. Woodland flowers including bluebells and wood anemones use its late-emerging canopy as proxy woodland in treeless areas. A lover of acidic, well-drained soils, it is particularly associated with pine trees and heather.

Just a whiff of its almondy scent instantly transports you to wild places. Strangely for such a tough plant, it rarely seems to grow in towns, so seeing bracken is for many of us the exclusive preserve of going on holiday or trips to the countryside.

In the Far East the young fronds (known as fiddleheads or fernbrakes in English) are eaten in many dishes, including Korean *bibimbap*. The rhizomes are a source of starch and used by many cultures across its native range, from North America to Europe and Japan. However, the plant is known to contain carcinogens, so its use in food is controversial, at least to many in the West.

If you do decide to tackle bracken, don't pull with bare hands, as it can cut you. Repeated treading down of the emerging fronds is an effective way to weaken and eventually kill bracken. Although it can be a weed in gardens, bracken still has its uses. Composted fronds can make a useful soil improver or garden mulch, while they can be used fresh or dried for animal bedding and an eco-friendly packing material.

Many of the plant's common names, along with its Latin epithet *aquilinum* (from *aquila*, or eagle) refer to the strange pattern that can be seen if you cut the base of the stem with a knife. This was likened to, among other things, a double-headed eagle and the initials of Jesus Christ.

{OPPOSITE} It might be common but bracken has a structural beauty that repays closer inspection

Ranunculus

Ranunculus acris (Meadow buttercup, tall buttercup), *R. bulbosus* (bulbous buttercup), *R. repens* (creeping buttercup)

Type of weed: Perennial
Family: *Ranunculaceae*
Uses: Ornamental
Poisonous: Yes

Simple and joyful – like a child's drawing of a flower, buttercups sprinkle our meadows, lawns and verges with gold. Their brilliant, pure yellow flowers are unashamed and abundant. They might be a humble, common flower but their bold coloration and reflectivity are the result of some pretty impressive engineering.

Buttercup petals have an extremely flat surface and a special double-layered structure that acts as a mirror, reflecting ultraviolet light to attract pollinating insects. The petal arrangement also acts as a parabolic mirror, reflecting infrared light to the centre of the flower, gently heating it to attract insects and increase the chance of fertilization.

Humans have been fascinated by the flowers' reflectivity for centuries, giving rise to the popular myth that holding a buttercup under your chin and seeing a reflection means you like butter. Sadly, all it really tells you is that you don't have a beard.

Similarly, reflective petals are found in celandines, which are members of the same family, *Ranunculaceae*, along with hellebores and clematis. *Ranunculus* comes from the Latin for "little frog", and like frogs, buttercups enjoy life in damp places.

Meadow buttercup is the tallest species, sometimes growing to 1m (3ft) or more. It favours heavy soils. Bulbous buttercup tolerates drier conditions than the others and, as a result,

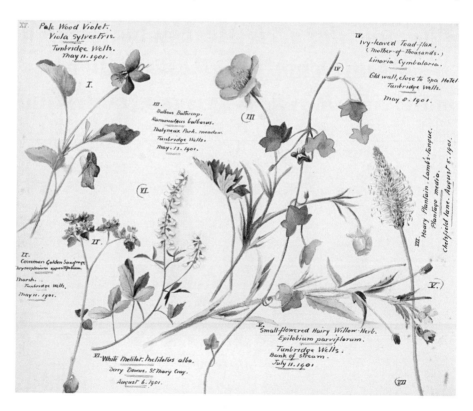

XV. Pale Wood Violet.
Viola Sylvestris.
Tunbridge Wells.
May 11. 1901.

I.

III.
Bulbous Buttercup.
Ranunculus bulbosus.
Molyneux Park. meadow.
Tunbridge Wells.
May. 13. 1901.

IV. Ivy-leaved Toad-flax.
(Mother-of-Thousands.)
Linaria Cymbalaria.
Old wall, close to Spa Hotel
Tunbridge Wells.
May 8. 1901.

IV.

III

VI.

II.

II.
Common Golden Saxifrage
Chrysosplenium oppositifolium.
Marsh.
Tunbridge Wells.
May 11. 1901.

VII. Hoary Plantain. Lamb's-tongue.
Plantago media.
Chelsfield lane. August 5. 1901.

V.

V. Small-flowered Hairy Willow-Herb.
Epilobium parviflorum.
Tunbridge Wells.
Bank of stream.
July 11. 1901.

VI. White Melilot. Melilotus alba.
Derry Downs. St Mary Cray.
August 6. 1901.

VII

is more common in southern and eastern England. Creeping buttercup, true to its name, creeps about, spreading by stolons (rather like strawberry plants do).

There are several cultivated varieties of meadow buttercup with double flowers that make beautiful and unusual garden plants. Their slender, airy growth and bright flowers mean they combine well with other plants such as Siberian iris. They retain the wild species' easy-going nature, but having double flowers means they're much less likely to seed about the place and make a nuisance of themselves. Cultivated forms of buttercups have been grown in gardens for a long time and have attracted some lovely, old-fashioned names over the years, including "fair maids of France" and "batchelor's buttons".

All species are toxic if eaten by either people or grazing animals. However, their bitter taste serves as a warning (the name *Ranunculus acris* refers to the plant's acrid taste), so cases of poisoning are rare. Also, the toxin is destroyed by drying, which explains why the plant's presence in hay meadows isn't seen as a problem.

Buttercups' abundant flowers are a mecca for all kinds of pollinating insects, from wild bees and hoverflies to butterflies and beetles. Peak flowering occurs in May–June, although creeping buttercup can keep on blooming as late as December.

Learning to use weeds as a tool to direct your gardening is a valuable skill. Creeping buttercup in your lawn is generally a sign

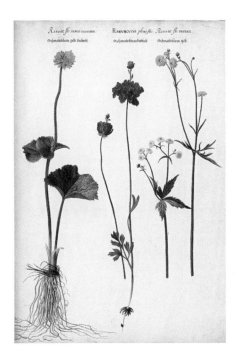

that it's too wet for short grass to thrive. This presents you with a choice: spray and drain it in pursuit of the perfect bowling green, killing the wildlife and making a lot of work for yourself in the process. Or, listen to what nature is telling you. Leave the mower in the shed and watch the lawn become a wildflower meadow studded with beautiful flowers and humming with life. Sometimes the most rewarding way of gardening is to let nature do it for you.

{OPPOSITE} Bulbous buttercup features prominently in this 1901 wildflower composite by Lilian Snelling

{ABOVE} There are cultivated forms of buttercup with double flowers

Reynoutria japonica
aka *Fallopia japonica*
Japanese knotweed

Type of weed: Perennial	
Family: *Polygonaceae*	
Uses: Edible, medicinal	
Poisonous: No	

Japanese knotweed is certainly striking: deep red shoots emerge in spring, quickly becoming dense leafy thickets of canes 1.8m (6ft) tall or more. Heart-shaped leaves grow in a zigzag pattern and the plants are festooned with sprays of small creamy-white flowers in autumn.

Writing in 1870, William Robinson, the great Victorian wild gardening pioneer, was rather enamoured with Japanese knotweed, calling it "very handsome indeed" and a "most effective flower in autumn". He also cautioned that the knotweed's shoots that "certainly can take care of themselves" – which in hindsight, something of an understatement. Just a few years later it escaped, and was reported growing wild on waste ground in south Wales in the 1880s. By the 1960s Japanese knotweed was growing wild right across the island, from Land's End to northern Scotland.

But what's the fuss about? As a contender for "worst weed", Japanese knotweed ranks pretty highly. It grows huge, pushing out other plants, it's hard to remove – and if you leave even the tiniest piece behind, it can re-establish. It can easily lift paving slabs and break through tarmac.

Eradication has been costed at £1.6 billion, requiring unsustainable amounts of pesticides, which is deemed unfeasible both financially and environmentally. Japanese knotweed is here to stay. Luckily, so far, knotweed mainly sticks to habitats shaped by humans, where human disturbance has left a gap – an ecological vacuum.

You could view it as nature's most strident first responder to the wounds left on the earth's surface by us. The plant's strongholds are mostly in urban areas, particularly along railway lines and where buildings have been demolished. In its natural habitat in Japan it's one of the first colonizers of fresh lava flows – kickstarting the long, slow process of turning barren black rock into fertile soil. Whether on a lava flow in Hokkaido or an abandoned car park in Hoxton, the same dynamic is at work.

Japanese knotweed is part of the *Polygonaceae* plant family, whose name means having many angles or many knees. Most have distinctive jointed stems, and Japanese knotweed is no exception. Other family members include rhubarb, buckwheat and docks. Look at the form of its stems and flowers, and you'll easily see its similarity to docks.

In common with some of its relatives, knotweed is both edible and nutritious, although it comes with caveats. In Japan the young shoots are consumed as a delicacy, and they're known to be healthy because they contain quantities of resveratrol (a compound with antioxidant properties that's also being investigated as a cancer treatment). However, it's technically illegal to transport knotweed without a licence (and don't, whatever you do, put knotweed kitchen scraps on your compost heap), and along with the possibility it will have been sprayed with herbicide, this is one wild food that's probably best left alone.

NB: Japanese knotweed is a genuine outlaw in the UK; planting it or causing it to grow in the wild is a criminal offence under the Wildlife and Countryside Act (1981). The best way to get rid of it is to call specialist contractors. Digging or cutting are inadvisable because they both risk spreading the plant further.

wild food that's probably best left alone.

Bees have no such worries, and they absolutely adore Japanese knotweed. It flowers at a useful time for them, helping to bridge the gap between summer wildflowers and the autumn ivy nectar flow. In the northwestern USA, Oregon knotweed honey is a speciality.

From destroying patios to contributing to the fight against cancer and helping our beleaguered bees, this is a complex, resilient, slightly terrifying plant, and one that deserves our respect if nothing else.

{ABOVE} Japanese knotweed's vigorous, elegant growth earned it a place in Victorian gardens

40

Rhododendron ponticum

Rhododendron ponticum, Pontic rhododendron

Type of weed: Shrub	
Family: *Ericaceae*	
Uses: Ornamental	
Poisonous: Yes	

Big, bold and beautiful – there's nothing subtle about
Rhododendron ponticum. It is a weedy supervillain, an
unequivocally invasive non-native to Britain.

O r is it non-native? Fossil evidence indicates that it grew naturally in Britain before the last Ice Age. Advancing ice sheets pushed it back to two isolated populations in the Iberian peninsula and Turkey; but there's an argument to say that it might have eventually got back to the UK anyway, had the English Channel not opened up.

It might seem difficult to imagine now, but rhododendrons were plant superstars in their day. In the late eighteenth and nineteenth centuries, increasing trade and commerce opened up the world and a flood of new plant introductions revolutionized gardening in Britain and Europe. Having the latest exotic plants was the height of fashion, and rhododendrons were particularly adored. They are pretty much the biggest, showiest evergreen shrubs you can grow outdoors. Today we take them for granted, but their impact on nineteenth-century gardeners was huge.

After many thousands of years' absence, *Rhododendron ponticum* arrived back in the UK in 1763. It proved an instant hit with the landed gentry, who planted it for pheasant cover on their estates. However, *R. ponticum* had other ideas and, like so many non-natives, after a few years of good behaviour to lull us all into a false sense of security, it jumped the estate boundaries and headed for the wider countryside.

What a jump it was! *Rhododendron ponticum* is now estimated to inhabit almost 100,000 hectares (250,000 acres) of woodland. Its reproductive capabilities are legendary. A single plant can, by rooting where its branches touch the soil, cover more than 100 square metres (1,076 sq ft). Plus it engages in chemical warfare (allelopathy) to subdue other plants nearby and produces copious tiny seeds that can travel a kilometre (⅔ mile) from the parent plant. The species has become a serious pest in wetter, western parts of Britain and Ireland, invading woodlands and crowding out other plants, as well as rare mosses and lichens.

The large purple flowers of *Rhododendron ponticum* are known as "forest roses" in the lush Black Sea forests of the Turkish part of its native range. Strangely, the nectar from some plants is poisonous. Although occasionally used for recreational purposes and sometimes considered an aphrodisiac, "Turkish mad honey" made by bees foraging on rhododendrons produces hallucinations, nausea, fainting and a host of other unpleasant symptoms. Luckily, though, this trait appears to be becoming less prevalent in invasive populations – about 20% of the plants now produce no toxins in their nectar at all.

Ecological considerations aside, these rhododendrons in full bloom are a glorious sight. They make evergreen, glossy-leaved shrubs up to 8m (26ft) tall, bearing large heads of pinkish-purple flowers in May and June. In common with other rhododendrons, they will only grow in acid soil. So if you see them locally, it means you can grow blueberries, heathers and camellias in your garden to your heart's content. *Rhododendron ponticum* is pretty much the only weed we call by its Latin name, which is perhaps a mark of grudging respect for this glamorous and beautiful menace.

{ABOVE} Bold, beautiful and bad,
Rhododendron ponticum is a true vegetable
vagabond outside its native habitat

41

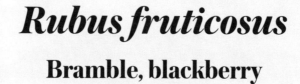

Rubus fruticosus

Bramble, blackberry

Type of weed:	Perennial
Family:	*Rosaceae*
Uses:	Edible, medicinal
Poisonous:	No

Brambles are perplexing plants. On the one hand,
they're generous providers of tasty fruit with many health-
giving properties – and on the other they're fearsomely
armed vegetable warriors, ready to scratch you to pieces
and take over your garden. If you take a step back, however,
and look at the bigger picture, those thorns have an
important ecological role to play.

Sometimes known as nature's barbed wire, brambles are impressively armoured. Even the backs of the leaves have thorns. This prickliness serves an important purpose: thorny bramble thickets are a haven for the small and the young things of this world. Small birds, mammals and even sapling trees find refuge in bramble patches, safe from predators and browsing animals. Hence the old saying "thorn is mother of the oak" – brambles are a key part of the natural regeneration of forests.

Vigorous, woody vines, brambles can grow to 3m (10ft) tall or more. Their hooked thorns help them climb and protect them from being eaten. In mild temperate areas they're often semi-deciduous, retaining some leaves in winter. In early summer they're covered in pretty pink or white flowers; five-petalled with lots of central stamens like miniature single roses, which shows their roots in the *Rosaceae*, or rose family.

Brambles are one of the reasons no one can quite put a figure on how many native plants there are in Britain and other temperate parts of Eurasia. Botanically speaking, they're as tangled as a bramble patch. Taxonomists struggle to agree exactly what's what, so *Rubus fruticosus* is classed as an "aggregate" species, being made up of more than 300 microspecies. You'll see this if you go bramble picking – the size, shape and taste of the fruits and the plants varies enormously.

Picking blackberries is pretty much our only commonplace wild food ritual. The fruits become slightly less glossy when fully ripe, but they don't last long before going squishy. According to legend, they must be picked before Michaelmas Day in September, as during that night the Devil passes and spits on the fruit. Whether drenched in the Devil's spit or not, they're certainly at their best in August in the northern hemisphere.

If birds always seem to get there first, it's worth knowing that you can pickle the green fruits or cook the red unripe ones to make coulis or compote. Alternatively, try growing your own: there are some huge-fruited but still very tasty varieties out there such as 'Karaka Black' and 'Black Butte'. There are some thornless ones too; these are useful in small gardens if you grow them on wires along a wall or fence to help make the most of space on the ground.

Blackberries are superbly healthy fruit, containing lots of antioxidants, fibre, vitamins C and K. They also contain chemicals that potentially offer protection against age-related and cardiovascular diseases, and reduce the risk of cancer. Luckily, they freeze brilliantly so you can make the most of a summer glut and add them to your diet year-round. For the less health-conscious, they make wonderful jams and jellies too. So next time you see a bramble patch, think of it less as a thorny mess and more of a wildlife-friendly larder.

{OPPOSITE} Brambles' pretty flowers are great for bees. Look closely and you can see they're in the rose family

42

Rumex

Rumex obtusifolius (broad-leaved dock), *Rumex crispus* (curled dock)

Type of weed: Perennial	
Family: *Polygonaceae*	
Uses: Edible, medicinal	
Poisonous: No	

Deep-rooted and tenacious, docks are some of nature's first responders when man messes things up. Craters of mud on building sites, roadworks, trodden-down soil that's too oxygen-starved to support much life at all… docks will be there. Their deep roots break through compacted layers of soil with amazing ease. When they eventually die, the field is opened up to all sorts of plants that couldn't have grown there before.

Docks have handsome rich green leaves, and are much loved for them. The cooling sensation of pressing a dock leaf to the skin, or the evaporative cooling from rubbing dock juice into a sting – or perhaps just the placebo effect – mean that many of us reach for a dock leaf when stung by a nettle. There doesn't seem to be any scientific evidence suggesting this is effective, but it's heartening to see a plant-based folk remedy surviving into the twenty-first century.

There's a quiet (if slightly terrifying) beauty in docks' petal-less flowers and seeds. As summer gathers pace, their greenish flower heads blush deep orange-red before fading to a rich brown. Look closely, and you'll see they have fruits like tiny three-sided lanterns, each containing a seed – if you're brave enough to let them get that far. Dock seeds can remain viable for 60 years or more, and although they're loved by birds they will often germinate in large quantities. Docks are also loved by many species of moths, whose caterpillars can decimate the foliage by late summer.

Both curled and broad-leaved dock can grow to around 4ft (1.2m) tall and their roots can go down 3ft (1m) into the soil. Members of the knotweed or buckwheat family (*Polygonaceae*), they are closely related to the herb sorrel. They're edible too, and if you nibble on them you'll instantly recognize the similarity in their sharp, lemony taste. Their leaves are full of vitamins and minerals – although they also contain oxalic acid, which means you shouldn't eat too much. If consumed to excess, the acid

Rumex obtusifolius.

{ABOVE} Docks are tough plants, and will bravely resist any attempt to pull or dig them up

{OPPOSITE} Surprisingly, docks are edible. They're closely related to the herb sorrel

can cause kidney damage and can aggravate gout and rheumatism. Young leaves can be steamed as greens or used in place of vine leaves for stuffing.

It's almost as if docks designed themselves to thwart any attempt at uprooting them. The weakest point is the join between the stem and the root: don't even think about trying to pull them up by hand. Their deep taproots mean you need a fork or spade to lever them out of the soil. Otherwise, the plant will simply snap, only to regrow rapidly into an even bigger

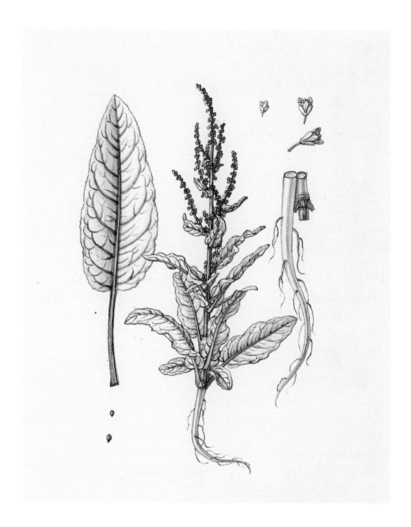

clump. Seedlings quickly develop a strong taproot so need to be individually uprooted, rather than being hoed off.

Docks' more refined relatives include red-veined sorrel (*Rumex sanguineus*), which is a pretty plant that crosses the boundaries between vegetable, garnish and herb. Bistort (*Persicaria superbum*) – the name of which has caused many a chortle in horticulture classes over the years – is a tough and dependable herbaceous perennial with pretty spikes of pink flowers in summer.

Senecio vulgaris

Groundsel

Type of weed: Annual	**Uses:** None
Family: *Asteraceae*	**Poisonous:** Yes

A tough little cookie, groundsel is often known as an ephemeral weed on account of its fast-paced lifestyle. In poor, dry soils during summer, it can germinate, flower and set seed in just a few weeks at only 8cm (3in) high, and can even set seed after it has been uprooted.

In common with many other weeds, groundsel has the amazing ability to tailor its growth and reproductive pattern to the prevailing conditions. When conditions are more favourable, it spends much longer growing and can more than quintuple in size to 45cm (18in). Generally preferring damp, rich soils, groundsel is one of a select group of plants that can grow and flower all year round, having multiple generations.

Despite its reproductive superpowers, *Senecio vulgaris* is not much of a looker. Its small yellow flower heads are generally made of just disc florets – like the centre of a sunflower or thistle flowers. These quickly turn into seed heads, which burst open to reveal copious seeds, each with a fluffy pappus – hairlike bristles that act as a parachute, enabling the seeds to travel long distances on the wind. This is a speciality of the *Asteraceae* (daisy) plant family, and can also be seen in thistledown and dandelion clocks.

A cosmopolitan bunch, *Asteraceae* is the world's biggest plant family. Within it, *Senecio* is a large genus, containing an amazing range of plants from groundsel and weedy Oxford ragwort (*Senecio squalidus*), to succulents such as the houseplant string of pearls (*Senecio rowleyanus*), to the incredible and eerie, giant groundsels (sometimes placed in the subgenus *Dendrosenecio*) which grow up to 10m (33ft) tall on the highest mountains of eastern Africa. The word *Senecio* comes from the Latin for "old man" – a reference to the copious grey fluffy seeds – and, perhaps slightly insensitively, the bald appearance of the remains of the seed head once they've blown away.

Once those seeds have landed, they do the classic weed trick of germinating quickly and looking inconspicuously similar to other things. The seedlings look superficially like young brassicas such as cabbage or rocket seedlings; the easiest way to tell them apart is to tear or crush a leaf and sniff it, as they lack the brassicas' sulphurous tang.

Pretty much the only thing that gardeners will see eating groundsel is the cinnabar moth (*Tyria jacobaeae*). Its stripy orange and black caterpillars are one of the few creatures that can tolerate the toxic alkaloids in the plants' leaves and will quite often totally destroy groundsel plants during the summer months before pupating to become pretty black and red moths.

Groundsel was formerly used as a medicinal "cure-all" for everything, from deworming children to curing scrofula (also known as "the king's evil", a nasty bacterial infection of the lymph nodes associated with tuberculosis). Sadly, modern medicine is yet to prove these treatments effective. If you don't fancy growing food for moths, groundsel is easily removed by hand as soon as it appears. To prevent it growing in the first place, use mulches and no-dig systems because these reduce soil disturbance, which is one of the main stimuli for groundsel.

{BELOW} Groundsel is a common weed of disturbed ground, such as vegetable patches

44

Solanum

Solanum dulcamara (woody nightshade, bittersweet), *Solanum nigrum* (black nightshade)

Type of weed:	Annual, perennial
Family:	*Solanaceae*
Uses:	None
Poisonous:	Yes

With their baleful presence and romantic, magical-sounding names, nightshades are an intriguing group of weeds. Two of them are common enough to turn up regularly in gardens. One is a bit of an ugly duckling, while the other is stunningly beautiful if you dare to look closely.

Both black nightshade (*Solanum nigrum*) and woody nightshade (*Solanum dulcamara*) contain the poison solanine, which is also what makes green potatoes poisonous. Ingestion can cause vomiting, paralysis, coma, and even death. The nightshade family, *Solanaceae*, seems to have a love-hate relationship with humans, containing many toxic plants along with important crops like potatoes, tomatoes and aubergines.

Black nightshade looks rather like a weedy aubergine plant, growing 20–60cm (8–24in) tall with soft green leaves and the family's distinctive flowers, starlike with a central point. It's a quick-growing annual and often one of the first colonizers of bare disturbed earth on building sites or when vegetation has been sprayed off. Its seeds can last for decades when buried, and its presence tends to indicate rich soil.

Solanum nigrum has many varieties and hybridizes readily with related species to form an extremely complex group of plants, with wildly varying levels of toxicity and edibility. Some are grown in West Africa as leaf crops, and there are edible varieties sometimes known as wonderberries. But from a European gardener's perspective it's very hard to shake off the association with the toxic wild black nightshade – and if you have this plant growing in your garden, don't try the cultivated sorts, as the wild ones could seed in there or cross with them.

If black nightshade is the beast, woody nightshade or bittersweet (*Solanum dulcamara*) is the beauty. A sprawling, semi-climbing herbaceous plant, it scrambles over hedgerows, scrubland, riverbanks and wilder parts of gardens. The purple and yellow flowers look like a multicoloured version of tomato flowers. Look closely, and you'll see exotic-looking bright green and white spots at the base of the petals. The flowers are followed by pretty traffic-light berries that start green, ripening through yellow and orange, to a very tempting scarlet – toxic to humans but a useful source of wild bird food.

If you appreciate the look of woody nightshade but not its weediness, and want something even prettier, try the potato vines, *Solanum jasminoides* and *S. laxum*. They're joyful plants, quick-growing and vigorous with abundant flowers in summer and early autumn.

Both nightshades have interesting reproductive habits. Pollen is a precious resource: the plant requires a lot of energy to make it, so nightshades go to incredible lengths to ensure as little as possible is wasted. Having evolved in tandem with bees for thousands upon thousands of years, nightshades decided that instead of offering a banquet of pollen laid out like many other more wasteful plants, they would shed their pollen through pores, only to be released by the buzz of bumblebees as they hang on to the flowers, contracting their flight muscles to reach just the right vibration. Once it hits the right note, a highly targeted explosion of pollen covers the lucky bee. Tomatoes share the same trait (compare their flowers, and their close family links become obvious), which is why bumblebees are bred in their millions to pollinate commercial tomato crops.

{OPPOSITE} Woody nightshade berries might look tasty but are best left for the birds – they are poisonous

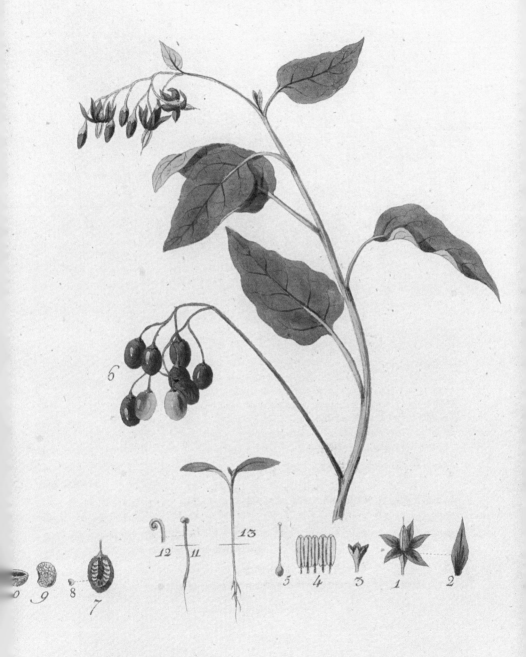

45

Stellaria media

Chickweed, starweed, winterweed, stitchwort

Type of weed:	Annual
Family:	*Caryophyllaceae*
Uses:	Edible, medicinal
Poisonous:	No

It might be thought of as a weed, but chickweed is quite simply one of the best wild greens out there. A very widely distributed plant, it has been traditionally eaten everywhere it grows, from England to Japan. Although the plants themselves are pretty flimsy, the seeds are light and incredibly tough: chickweed is now found on every inhabited continent.

Stellaria media is a low-growing annual with bright green, oval pointed leaves and lax growth 5–40cm (2–16in) high. Its scrambling, brittle stems have a line of hairs down one side. If you look under a magnifying glass, you'll see the tiny starry white flowers have five petals, each divided like bunny ears to give the impression of there being 10. The Latin name *Stellaria* comes ultimately from *stella* or star, referring to the shape of the flowers.

But back to those leaves. They're not just edible but genuinely tasty, with a sweet, slightly nutty flavour. Chickweed is very nutritious; rich in vitamins (especially vitamins C and A) and minerals such as iron and calcium. Once you've tried eating these leaves, you'll think it's madness to weed the plant out, only to go and buy a bagged-up salad that's been driven hundreds of miles on a fume-belching lorry. Harvest only the tops of the plants to avoid the stringy lower stems – the best quality growth for eating is produced in the cooler months. Either use in mixed salads or on its own, chopped roughly and dressed with a vinaigrette. Or, if you have a lot, try making a soup, much like watercress or spinach soup. Just be aware that excessive consumption can cause laxative effects. Herbalists have used chickweed for centuries for its soothing, cooling and itch-relieving properties in poultices, infusions and ointments.

Chickweed can grow throughout the year, but its speciality is winter. It's one of our "winter weeds" – plants that will germinate in autumn and grow through the winter, taking advantage of any mild spells and the lack of competition from other plants. In optimum conditions, plants can mature and set seed in just over a month; chickweed is capable of five generations a year! Generally its presence is an indicator of fertile soil.

The main enemy of chickweed is the hoe. It can produce thousands and thousands of seedlings; luckily, they're fragile and can be dealt with very easily. Alternatively, mulching will discourage it, as it needs open, bare soil to thrive. Chickens, as you might expect from the plant's name, adore chickweed and will happily control it for you.

Although sometimes called stitchwort, this name generally refers to a different woodland flower, *Stellaria holostea*, which is much bigger, making a pretty starlike display of white flowers in hedges, woods and shady gardens around bluebell time. They're both members of the pink or carnation family, *Caryophyllaceae*.

{OPPOSITE AND BELOW}
Chickweed's soft leaves are a
tasty wild food with a pleasant
nutty flavour

46

Taraxacum officinale

Dandelion, lion's teeth,
pee-the-bed, clocks

Type of weed:	Perennial
Family:	*Asteraceae*
Uses:	Edible, medicinal, ornamental
Poisonous:	No

When you consider dandelions' edible,
medicinal and wildlife value, it seems incredible
that we think of them as weeds at all. Look at
them with unbiased eyes and they're
rather beautiful too.

A long with daisies and celandines, dandelions are one of nature's most joyful ways to announce spring. Sheets of yellow flowers erupt on lawns and verges, shining brightly and alive with the sound of happy bees feasting on their abundant nectar, putting winter firmly to bed.

Pull a dandelion flower apart, and you'll see it's actually made of hundreds of individual flowers all clustered together. They are what's known as composite flowers, and are typical of the daisy family, *Asteraceae* (sometimes called

the *Compositae*) – and are very similar to their cousins the sow thistles (*Sonchus*, page 54). Having so many flowers packed tightly together makes them rich in pollen and nectar – a real boon for bees.

What starts as a boon for bees quickly becomes a bane for gardeners. Lots of flowers means lots of seeds, and dandelions are beautifully designed to waft away on the slightest breeze to settle in new places. Each seed has its own stalked parachute (technically known as a

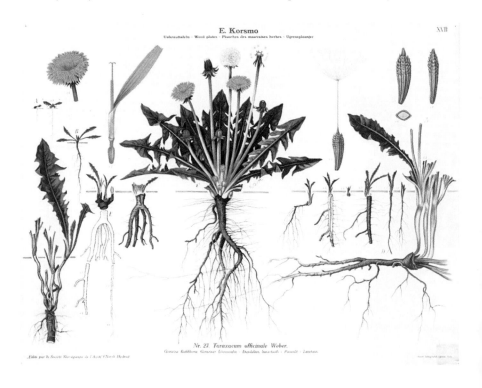

E. Korsmo   XVII
Unkrauttafeln · Weed plates · Planches des mauvaises herbes · Ugræsplansjer

Nr. 27 *Taraxacum officinale* Weber.
Gemeine Kuhblume. Gewöhner Løvetann · Dandelion, hawksbit · Pissenlit · Løvetann.

pappus), which is what we see when blowing the seed heads as a dandelion "clock".

The name "dandelion" comes from the French *dent de lion* (lion's tooth), although no one is quite sure why. In France it's generally called "pissenlit" which relates back rather forthrightly to the old English name of pee-the-bed. Despite their less than appealing local moniker, dandelions are loved in France, where they're grown as an edible crop. Plants are blanched or forced, much like rhubarb: by excluding light, the leaves become less bitter and more tender, making them especially good to eat raw in salads.

You can use dandelion as a substitute for radicchio in salad recipes. Young green leaves work particularly well with sweet salad dressings based on maple syrup or honey. Alternatively, more mature leaves and flowers can be deep fried in batter – their bitterness is a good match for oily recipes.

Dandelion leaves are incredibly healthy, being full of vitamins A, B, C, D and minerals. Just avoid them before bedtime; as the old names suggest they are an effective diuretic. Dandelion also assists liver and kidney function, along with digestion. Harvest away from areas with farm animals, dog-walking paths and anywhere that might have been sprayed with weedkiller.

An abundance of dandelions indicates that you have rich soil. If you want to make the most of dandelion's many uses, plant pieces of root in the vegetable patch. The more generously you

treat them, the more they'll give. You can even harvest the flower buds for pickling (they make a useful homegrown caper substitute) and they won't seed around.

It really is amazing when you take a closer look – this common weed that we spend so long trying to get rid of is edible top to toe, has many medicinal properties and wildlife loves it, too. Does it even deserve to be called a weed?

{OPPOSITE} Dandelions' strong roots are their secret weapon. They can regrow from even tiny fragments

{ABOVE} The name dandelion comes from the French for "lion's tooth"

Trifolium

Trifolium pratense (Red clover), *Trifolium repens* (white clover, bee-bread)

Type of weed:	Perennial
Family:	*Leguminosae*
Uses:	Edible, ornamental
Poisonous:	No

There are many, many reasons why we should liberate clovers from their classification as weeds. Clovers will feed your soil for free, feed the bees and keep your lawn green in a drought. And if that's not enough, you can eat them too!

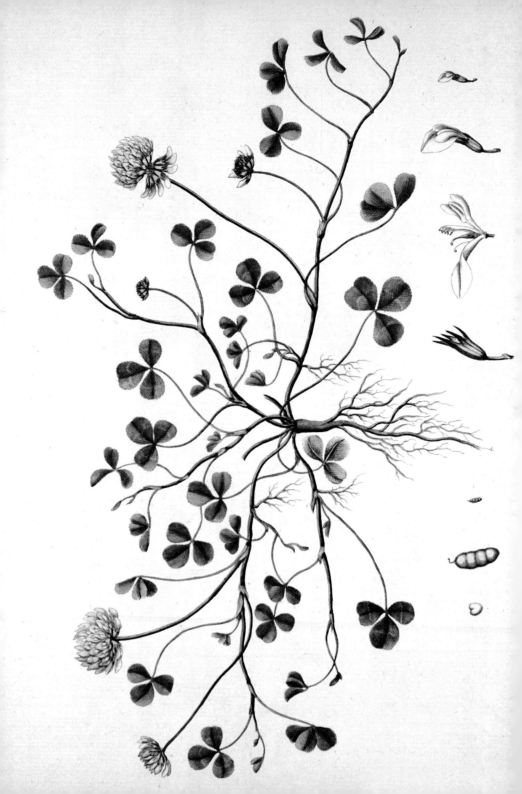

Among our many native species, two are common enough in gardens to sometimes be thought of as weeds. Red clover is the taller of the two, growing to around 60cm (2ft). It lights up long grass and meadows for months on end with its rich pink flower heads, and has a distinctive pale "V" on its leaves. White clover is shorter (its Latin name *repens* means "creeping") and is more at home in lawns and paths. It grows to a maximum height of around 45cm (18in), although it's often much shorter and is fantastically adapted to living in lawns. The leaves are rounder, usually with pale markings.

Both are much loved by bees. The deep flowers of red clover attract many bumblebees (their tongues are long enough to reach the nectar within), while white clover is loved by honeybees and solitary bees. According to a recent study, white clover, thistles and heather together provide an astonishing 50% of our national nectar provision. You can get a taste of clover's sweet abundance for yourself by pulling off the individual flowers and sucking them for a drop of sweet nectar. The young tender leaves can be eaten too. Clover's Latin name means three leaves (*tri-folium*). However, sometimes you'll find variants with four leaves, which are deemed lucky. According to folklore, finding a four-leaf clover enables you to see fairies!

Clovers are what's known as legumes, being in the *Leguminosae* or pea family, and in common with the rest of their kin they have the ability to "fix" nitrogen from the air. Nitrogen is an incredibly important element for plants; it's what keeps them green and healthy. Humans discovered how to make artificial nitrogen fertilizer just over 100 years ago and it's now one of the most environmentally damaging things we do. It causes about 1% of all human emissions of carbon dioxide, along with widespread water pollution caused by the run-off of excess fertilizer.

However, when clovers fix nitrogen, they run on sunlight and make no pollution at all. They form a symbiotic relationship with a soil bacterium (*Rhizobium*), which invades the roots and forms nodules. Within the nodules the bacteria get to work, transforming inert nitrogen gas (78% of the atmosphere) into ammonia which plants use as fertilizer.

Synthetic, ammonia-based, nitrogen fertilizer is one of the main components of most lawn feeds. Why not ditch the chemicals and let nature do the work? Allowing clover into your lawn is a good idea on so many levels. Your lawn will feed itself, helping the environment and saving you cash, and it will even stay greener for longer during drought conditions. And, of course, the bees will thank you, too. Whoever said clover was a weed?

{OPPOSITE} Small-leaved clovers make a valuable addition to lawns as they help keep the grass looking green all year round

48

Urtica dioica
Stinging nettle

Type of weed: Perennial	
Family: *Urticaceae*	
Uses: Edible, medicinal	
Poisonous: No	

Nettles are incredible plants. Few other species have such a range of uses. A source of food, medicine, fibre and fertilizer, *Urtica dioica* even has some impressive wildlife-supporting credentials too.

Stand close to nettles and take in their tangy, hedgerow scent. Green and refreshing with a hint of elderflower, it's the essence of outdoors and country walks. Growing between 30cm (1ft) and 5ft (1.5m) tall, nettles have tough, fibrous roots and stems. They laugh in the face of danger, growing back quickly after flood or fire.

Our language shows that we have a love-hate relationship with this most useful plant. "Nettlesome" is an old-fashioned word for irritating, while a "nettler" is an irritating or aggravating person or thing. But does it deserve such bad press?

The history of nettles is woven into human history. They appear in placenames in almost every county in England, from Nettlestead in Kent to Nettlepot in County Durham, which just shows how important they can be.

Their use as fabric goes back to the Vikings and beyond, way before the introduction of cotton from the tropics. You can make your own nettle plant ties by harvesting plants when they're about 1m (3ft) tall; wearing leather gloves, pull the stems through your clenched fist to remove leaves and stings, then split them open lengthwise and remove the central pith. You'll now have just the fibre, ready to be split again into strips and plaited together. It's surprisingly strong and handy for all sorts of jobs, like tying in your tomatoes.

The Latin name *Urtica dioica* refers to the fact that the plants are dioecious, meaning separate males and females, like hollies and asparagus plants. If you watch a nettle patch in flower on a still summer day, you'll see nettle sex in action, as the male plants release puffs of yellowish pollen into the air in the hope that some will land on receptive female flowers.

Nettles are a superb aphid and caterpillar plant. So what? Well, we're used to thinking of krill or plankton as being the basis of the ocean food chain, supporting everything from sardines to sperm whales. Aphids and caterpillars are the same on land. Bring them in and suddenly there's food for blue tits, ladybirds and a host of other creatures. Nettles are also the larval food plant for peacock, red admiral and small tortoiseshell butterflies – look out for the caterpillars' distinctive cobwebby tents.

Nettles are nourishing for people too. Their leaves are rich in vitamins A and C, along with protein, omega 3, iron and calcium. Eat only the young leaves; the best pickings are in spring as they emerge. Add to soups, pesto, pasta, risottos – they only really need wilting to make them edible and retain their nutritional value. Nettles have anti-inflammatory properties and can make a tonic for hair or oily skin. They are also a traditional remedy for arthritis.

A wonderful tonic they may be, but you can have too much of a good thing. Don't consume either the tea or the leaves to excess, and don't eat them when the plant is flowering or is growing on manure heaps because they become too high in nitrogen for our bodies to handle. If your nettle patch (or addiction) has gone too far, you can make a superb organic liquid feed by chopping and soaking them in water until it's the colour of weak tea.

Whether you use them to feed yourself, feed your plants, make fibre or just leave them alone for the wildlife, nettles are one weed that earns its keep.

{ABOVE} Nettles are among the most
useful of weeds, for both people and wildlife

Veronica

Arvensis (Corn speedwell, wall speedwell), *V. filiformis* (slender speedwell), *V. hederifolia* (ivy-leaved speedwell), *V. chamaedrys* (germander speedwell) and others

Type of weed: Annual, perennial	
Family: *Plantaginaceae*	
Uses: Ornamental	
Poisonous: No	

A beautiful mystery. "Speedwells are roadside plants which speed you on your journey," says eminent nature writer Richard Mabey in *Flora Britannica*. Yet nobody knows why. Perhaps it is just their simple beauty, which would have been much more noticeable in the slower-paced days before cars.

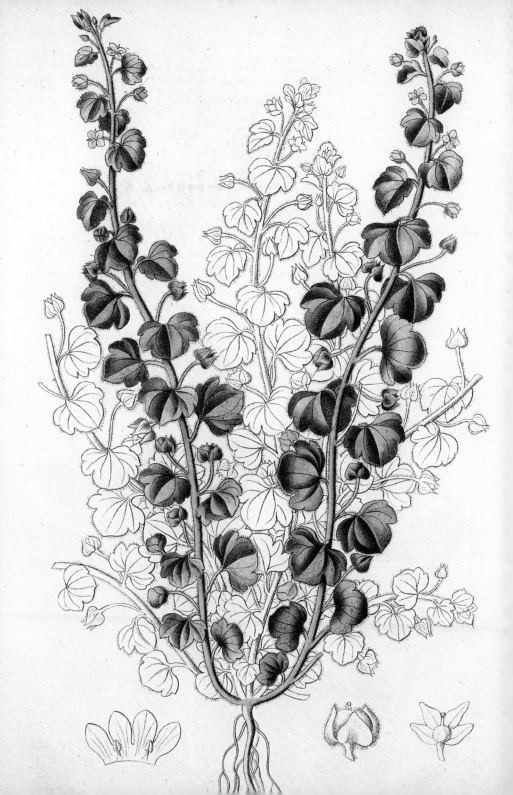

Germander speedwell (*Veronica chamaedrys*), in particular, was sewn into travellers' clothes or worn as a good luck charm. Today it's little known, except to the more mean-spirited lawn purists who call it a stubborn weed. Yet there's much to be gained from taking time to slow down, look closely and appreciate the small and wild things in life. The overall winner of a recent RHS Photographic Competition was an image of this speedwell, its dainty flowers glowing a rich blue in the dappled sunlight of a spring morning. Proof, if ever it were needed, that beauty is where you find it.

Our wild speedwells comprise around 15 relatively similar species of low-growing, blue-flowered sprawling plants. Most are native, although the most common, slender speedwell (*Veronica filiformis*) is from southeastern Europe. Introduced as a rock garden plant in the 1800s, it very quickly decided it was much more at home in lawns. Just like pineapple weed (see page 124) it's quite a fan of human technology, and found itself in the right place at the right time. Within 200 years it has spread far and wide, and is now found right across the landscape, apart from the highest mountains.

Why such a rapid and total spread? The blame (if you can call spreading such a pretty flower a crime) can be laid squarely at the foot of one Mr Budding, who in 1830 invented the lawnmower. As a piece of equipment, lawnmowers might as well have been designed as a speedwell-spreading tool. *Veronica filiformis* and its kin can regenerate from even tiny fragments, so finely chopped lawn clippings are the perfect way to make more of them, either within the lawn or if the clippings are spread as mulch.

Look closely into its baby blue flowers, so pure, so beautiful. It's difficult to believe that anyone would douse them in weedkillers. But they have – and it has become resistant to almost all of them. Small and dainty, but tough as old boots: slender speedwell has the last laugh.

If you have speedwell in your garden, you might as well learn to love it. After all, blue flowers are relatively rare and many gardeners treasure them. There are many cultivated veronicas available too: try the prostrate speedwell, *Veronica prostrata*, or the lovely cultivated variety *Veronica* 'Shirley Blue' – they're both trouble-free plants with delightful blue flowers that will bring bees and butterflies to your garden.

{OPPOSITE} Attractive and dainty, speedwells such as this *Veronica hederifolia* repay a closer look

{BELOW} Pure blue flowers are relatively rare in nature, although many *Veronica* species have them

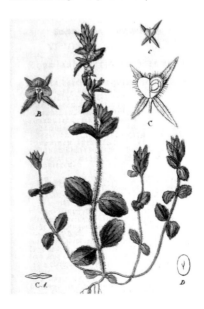

50

Vicia

Vicia sativa (common vetch), *Vicia hirsuta* (hairy vetch, hairy tare)

Type of weed: Annual	
Family: *Leguminosae*	
Uses: Edible	
Poisonous: Uncooked seeds are toxic	

"Scrambling" is a lovely word and it is beautifully apt for the way vetches grow – not quite climbing, not quite trailing. Their flexible wiry stems slip through, between and over other plants, covering them in a tangle of delicately divided leaves and pretty little flowers. A particular feature of vetches is that their leaves end in tendrils.

B ut what are they? As ever, it helps to consider the Latin name: *Vicia* is the same as broad beans (*Vicia faba*) – take a close look at the flowers, and instantly you'll see how they're related, not only to broad beans but also to peas and sweet peas. They're all members of the legume family, or *Leguminosae*, and can make their own nitrogen fertilizer (see also clover page 184).

Vicia hirsuta translates as hairy vetch (*hirsuta* as in hirsute). The species name of common vetch, *sativa*, translates as cultivated: the plant has been grown so widely and for so long that no one is really sure where it's native to. Which goes a long way towards showing what a useful plant it is.

Common vetch was formerly widely grown as a fodder crop for livestock. In the days before fertilizers became cheap and plentiful, its habit of enriching the soil as it grows was very useful. You can still buy common vetch seeds for use as a green manure – it is generally sold as "winter tares" and used as a tough crop to cover the soil over the colder months. Sow densely in August or September and they'll smother all the weeds. To get the maximum fertilizer value, dig in before the plants set seed, although it's worth leaving a patch to flower and watch the bees come flocking in.

Common vetch is so keen to help out that along with its abundant pollen-rich flowers it even produces "extrafloral nectaries" – even more nectar in drops along stems. This is thought to encourage ants, which then defend the plant against attack from herbivores. Hairy vetch produces copious nectar too, so much so

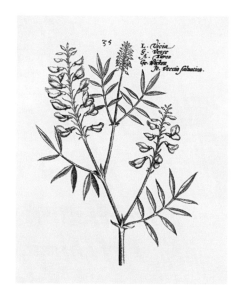

that the flowers almost drip with it, making it a mecca for all sorts of pollinating insects. Hairy vetch grows to about 45cm (18in) and common vetch to around 1m (3ft) tall, although both will be much smaller in dry places and where there's lots of competition.

The seeds are technically edible, given the right preparation. Hairy vetch has been used as a lentil substitute, although the word "substitute" probably tells you all you need to know. One charming old name is "poor man's peas". In common with many other legumes such as kidney beans, the seeds need thorough soaking and cooking in changes of water to make them edible. They're tiny, though, and really not worth it – grow vetches for free fertilizer and for the wonderful wildlife they bring in instead.

{OPPOSITE} Vetches were well known
in ancient times as common weeds of
arable crops

{ABOVE} The flowers of vetches resemble
miniature sweet peas

Index

(numbers in *italic* refer to captions)

A

absinthe 30
abutilons 122
Acer pseudoplatanus (sycamore) 7,
  8–11
Achillea millefolium (yarrow) 7,
  12–15, 111, *199*
Achilles 14
adder's root, *see* cuckoo pint
Aegopodium podagraria (ground
  elder) 16–19
  'Variegatum' 19
aggregate species 162–5
Amaranthaceae family 50–3
Anagallis arvensis (scarlet pimper-
  nel) 20–3
Anagallis monellii 22–3
Anchusa ('Loddon Royalist') 135
anthuriums 35
Apiaceae family 96–9
Araceae family 116–19, *118*
Araliaceae family 92–5
Arctium (burdock) 24–7
Artemisia absinthium (wormwood)
  30
Artemisia dracunculus (tarragon) 30
Artemisia vulgaris (mugwort) 28–31
Arum italicum (Italian arum) 35
Arum maculatum (cuckoo pint)
  32–5
Asparagaceae family 100–3
Asteraceae family 6, 14, 24–7, 27,
  108–11, 170–1, 180–3
  Achillea millefolium (yarrow)

13–15
Arctium 24–7
Artemisia vulgaris (mugwort)
  28–31
Bellis perennis (daisy) 36–9
Cirsium; Sonchus (thistles) 54–7
Matricaria discoidea (pineapple
  weed) 124–7
aubretia 49

B

Balsaminaceae family 104–7
batchelor's buttons 153
bathua, see fat hen
'Beacon Silver' deadnettle 114
bedstraw 76–9
bee-bread 184–7
bee bums 104–7
beetroot 52
Bellis perennis (daisy) 36–9
bibimbap 149
bindweed 7, 42–5, 76
bishop weed 16–19
bistort 169
bittercress 46–9
bittersweet 172–5
black bindweed 45
'Black Butte' blackberry 165
black nightshade 172–5
blackberry 67, 76, 162–5
bleeding hearts 144
bloody fingers, *see* cuckoo pint
blue corydalis 144
bluebell 100–3, 149

bombweed 66–9
borage 135
Boraginaceae family 132–5
bottle-brush 73
bracken/brackenfern 146–9
bramble 67, 76, 162–5
bras 170
Brassicaceae family 49, 170
'Brazen Hussy' celandine 75
British Beekeepers Association
  (BBA) 106
broad bean 198
broad-leaved dock (*Rumex*) 166–9
broadleaf plantain 136–7
buckwheat 156, 168
Budding, Mr 195
buddleia 6, 40–1
Buddleja davidii (buddleia) 6, 40–1
bulbous buttercup 150–3
burdock 24–7, 79
burrs 27
Burton, Tim 60
busy lizzies 106
buttercup 7, 74–5, 150–3
'Buttercup' ivy 95
butterfly bush 6, 40–1
Butterfly Conservation 40

C

cabbage 49, 170
cacti 119
Calystegia sepium (hedge bindweed)
  42–5
caper 183

Caprifoliaceae family, *Dipsacus* (teasle) 58–61
Carboniferous period 73
Cardamine hirsuta (bittercress) 46–9
cardamom 127
Carex (sedge) 86
carrot family, *see Apiaceae* family
Caryophyllaceae family 176–9
celandine 74–5, 152
Celtic white herb robert 87
Chamerion angustifolium (rosebay willowherb) 66–9
chamomile 127
Chatto, Beth 6
Chaucer, Geoffrey 38
Chelsea Flower Show 73
Chenopodium album (fat hen) 50–3
chickweed 176–9
Chinese medicine 27
chrysanthemum 127
cinnabar moth (*Tyria jacobaeae*) 110–11, 170–1
Cirsium arvense (creeping thistle) 54, 56
Cirsium palustre (marsh thistle) 54, 56
Cirsium rivulare 'Atropurpureum' (plume thistle) 56
Cirsium (thistle) 54–7
Cirsium vulgare (spear thistle) 54, 56
Clare, John 110
clarkia 67
cleavers 76–9

clematis 152
clocks 180–3
clove root, *see* herb bennett
clover 7, 184–7
cocoa 122
Code of Practice on How to Prevent the Spread of Ragwort (Defra) 111
coffee family 79
comfrey 135
common duckweed 116–19
common ivy 92–5
common mallow 120–3
common ragwort 108–11
common vetch 196–9
Compositae family, *see Asteraceae* family
composite flowers 38, 182
Convolvulus 7
Convolvulus (bindweed) 42–5
Convolvulus cneorum 45
Convulvulaceae family:
corn speedwell 192–5
cornbine, *see* field bindweed
Corydalis lutea (yellow corydalis) 142–5
Corydalis 'Tory MP' (true-blue corydalis) 144
couch grass 62–5
cow parsley *19*
cows and bulls, *see* cuckoo pint
cranesbill 80–3
creeping buttercup 7, 150–3
creeping thistle 54, 56
croziers 149
Cruciferae family, *see Brassicaceae*

family
cuckoo pint 32–5
curled dock (*Rumex*) 166–9

D

daisy family, *see Asteraceae* family
dandelion 7, 170, 180–3
day's eyes 38
deadnettle 112–15
Defra 111
Dendrosenecio subgenus 170
Dennstaedtiaceae family 146–9
devil's guts, *see* field bindweed
Devonian period 73
Dicentra (bleeding hearts) 144
dinosaurs 70, 73
Dipsacus (teasle) 58–61
disc flowers, described 127
dock (*Rumex*) 6, 156, 166–9
dog's dibble, *see* cuckoo pint
dove's foot cranesbill 80–3
dovesfoot geranium 80–3
duckweed 116–19
dwarf mallow 122

E

Elymus repens (couch grass) 62–5
English bluebell 100–3
English daisy 36–9
English ivy 92–5
Epilobium angustifolium 'Album' (white willowherb) 67
Epilobium (rosebay willowherb) 66–9

Equisetaceae family, *Equisetum arvense* (horsetail) 70–3
Equisetum arvense (horsetail) 70–3
Ericaceae family 158–61
Erigeron karavinskianus (Mexican fleabane) 38
evening primrose 67
evergreen bugloss 132–5

F

fair maids of France 153
Fallopia convolvulus (black bindweed) 45
Fallopia japonica (Japanese knotweed) 154–7
fat hen 50–3
fennel 98
fern allies 73
fernbrakes 149
ferns 146–9
Ficaria verna (lesser celandine) 74–5
fiddleheads 149
field bindweed 7, 42–5
fig buttercup 74–5
fireweed 66–9
First World War 67
Flora Britannica 192
forest rose, *see* rhododendron
forget-me-not 135
'Frances Perry' Welsh poppy 130
fronds 149
fuchsia 67
Fuller's teasel 58–61
Fumaria (fumitory) 144

G

Galium aparine (cleavers) 76–9
Garden Butterfly Survey 40
gaura 67
Geraniaceae family:
    Geranium molle (dove's foot cranesbill) 80–3
    Geranium robertianum (herb robert) 84–7
geranium 80–3, 84–7
Gerard, John 67
germander speedwell 192–5
Geum rivale (water aven) 90
Geum urbanum (herb bennett) 88–91
giant fennel 98
giant groundsel 170
giant hog fennel 98
giant hogweed 96–9
goat weed 16–19
gobo 27
goosefoot 50–3
goosegrass 76–9
greater burdock, *see* burdock
green alkanet 132–5
ground elder 16–19
groundsel 170–1

H

hairy bittercress 46–9
hairy tare 196–9
hairy vetch 196–9
hardy cranesbills *82*, 86, *87*
Harry Potter 132, 173
heal-all 138–41
Hedera helix (ivy) 92–5
hedge bindweed 42–5

hellebore 152
Heracleum (hogweed) 96–9
herb bennett 88–91
herb robert 82, 84–7
herba benedicta, *see* herb bennett
heuchera 86
hibiscus 122
Himalayan balsam 6, 98, 104–7
hogweed *19*, 96–9
hollyhocks 122
honeysuckle 60, 114
    family, *see Caprifoliaceae* family
horsetail 70–3, 79
hosta 86
Hyacinthoides (bluebell) 100–3
hybrid bluebell 100–3

I

Indian balsam 104–7
Impatiens glandulifera (Himalayan balsam) 104–7
Impatiens tinctoria 106
Industrial Revolution 67
Invasive Alien Species (Enforcement and Permitting) Order (2019) 98, 106
Ipomoea (morning glories) 45, *45*
Italian arum 35
ivy 92–5
ivy-leaved speedwell 192–5

J

Jacobaea vulgaris (ragwort) 108–11
Japanese knotweed 6, 154–7
Japanese maple 7
jewelweed 104–7

K

'Karaka Black' blackberry 165
Kew Gardens 124, 127
Knautia macedonica 60
Knepp Castle 57
knotweed 6, 154–7, 168

L

lady's bedstraw 79
lamb's cress 46–9
lambsquarters 50–3
Lamiaceae family 112–15, 138–41
Lamium (deadnettle) 112–15
Lamprocapnos (bleeding hearts) 144
land cress 46–9
lawn daisy 36–9
Leguminosae family 184–7, 196–9
Lemna minor (common duckweed) 116–19
lemongrass 127
lesser burdock, *see* burdock
lesser celandine 74–5
lion's teeth 180–3
living fossils, *see* horsetail
Lloyd, Christopher 74–5
'Loddon Royalist' 135
loosestrife 22
lords-and-ladies 32–5
Luzula (wood rush) 86
Lysimachia 22

M

Mabey, Richard 6, 103, 192
mallow 120–3
Malva sylvestris (common mallow)
120–3
Malvaceae family 120–3
mare's fart 108–11
mare's tail 70–3
marsh thistle 54, 56
Matricaria discoidea (pineapple weed) 124–7
meadow buttercup 150–3
meadow cranesbill 86
Meconopsis cambrica (pani Cymraeg; Welsh poppy) 128–31
Mestral, George de 27
Mexican fleabane 38
mint family, *see Lamiaceae* family
Monstera deliciosa (Swiss cheese plant) 35, 118
'Moonshine' yarrow 111
morning glories 7, 45, *45*
muggert 28–31
mugwort 28–31
musk mallow 122
mustard 49
Myosotis (forget-me-not) 135

N

naked boys, *see* cuckoo pint
NASA 27, 95
National Herb Committee 65
nettle 113, 168, 188–91 (*see also* deadnettle)
nightshade 172–5

O

Oenothera (evening primrose) 67
oilseed rape 49
okra 122
Onagraceae family 66–9

Oppenheimer, Strilli 45
'Orion' cranesbill 82
Owen, Denis 40
Owen, Dr Jennifer 40
Oxford ragwort 170

P

pani Cymraeg 128–31
Papaver cambricum (pani Cymraeg; Welsh poppy) 128–31
Papaver cambricum var. *aurantiacum* 130
Papaveraceae family 128–31, 142–5
pappus 183
pea family, *see Leguminosae* family
peace lily 35, 118
pee-the-bed 180–3
Pentaglottis sempervirens (green alkanet) 132–5
Persicaria superbum (bistort) 169
Peucedanum verticillare (giant hog fennel) 98
Phillpotts, Eden 7
phytoremediation 119
pilewort 74–5
pineapple weed 124–7
Plantaginaceae family 136–7, 192–5
Plantago major 'Bowles' Variety' 137
Plantago major (broadleaf plantain) 136–7
Plantago major 'Rubrifolia'/'Rosularis' (rose plantain) 137
plantain 6, 136–7
plume thistle 56
Poaceae family, *Elymus repens* (couch grass) 62–5

policeman's helmet 104–7
Polygonaceae family 154–7, 166–9, 168
pontic rhododendron 158–61
poor-man's tobacco 28–31
poor man's weather vane, *see* scarlet pimpernel
poppy family, *see Papaveraceae* family
potato vine 174
Primulaceae family, *Anagallis arvensis* 21–3
prostrate speedwell 195
Prunella grandiflora (large-flowered self-heal) 140–1
Prunella vulgaris (self-heal) 138–41
Pseudofumaria lutea (yellow corydalis) 142–5
Pteridium aquilinum (bracken) 146–9
pteridophytes 73

Q

quackgrass 62–5
quinoa 52

R

ragwort 108–11, 170
Ragwort Control Act (2003) 111
Ranunculaceae family 74–5, 150–3
Ranunculus (buttercup) 150–3
Ranunculus ficaria (fig buttercup), *see Ficaria verna* (lesser celandine)
ray flowers, described 127
rayless mayweed 124–7
red clover 184–7
red deadnettle 112–15
Reynoutria japonica (Japanese knotweed) 154–7
Rhizobium 187
rhizomes 65, 149
rhododendron 158–61
Rhododendron ponticum (rhododendron) 158–61
RHS Award of Garden Merit 23, 35, 40
RHS Chelsea Flower Show 73
RHS Photographic Competition 195
RHS Plant Finder 14
rhubarb 156
Robinson, William 130, 156
rock fumewort 142–5
rocket 49, 170
Rosaceae family:
  Geum urbanum (herb bennett) 88–91
  Rubus fruticosus agg. 162–5
rose plantain 137
rose (*Rosaceae*) 88–91, 90, 162–5
rosebay willowherb 66–9
rosemary 113
rough horsetail 73
roundleaf mallow 122
'Rozanne' cranesbill 82
Rubiaceae family 76–9
Rubus fruticosus (bramble) 67, 76, 162–5
Rumex (dock) 166–9
Rumex sanguineus (sorrel) 168, 169

S

salvia 113
samaras *11*
Sapindaceae family 8–11
scabious 60
scarlet pimpernel 20–3
scouring rush 70–3
Scrophulariaceae family, *Buddleja davidii* (buddleia) 40–1
scutch 62–5
"second spring" 79
Second World War 65, 67
sedge 86
self-heal 138–41
Senecio jacobaea (ragwort) 108–11
Senecio rowleyanus (string of pearls) 170
Senecio squalidus (Oxford ragwort) 170
Senecio vulgaris (groundsel) 170–1
Shakespeare, William 11
shepherd's sundial, *see* scarlet pimpernel
shepherd's weather-glass, *see* scarlet pimpernel
Sissinghurst Garden 67
slender speedwell 192–5
small-leaved clover 187
smooth sow thistle 56
Snelling, Lilian *153*
Solanaceae family 172–5
Solanum jasminoides/laxum (potato vines) 174
Solanum (nightshade) 172–5
Sonchus oleraceus (smooth sow thistle) 56
Sonchus (thistle) 54–7, 182
sorrel 168, 169
sow thistle 54, 56, *57*, 182
Spanish bluebell 100–3
Spathiphyllum (peace lily) 35, 118
spear thistle 54, 56
speedwell 192–5
spinach 52, 178

spotted deadnettle 114
squitch grass 62–5
starweed 176–9
Stellaria media (chickweed) 176–9
stickyweed 76–9
stinging nettle 113, 168, 188–91
stinking bob 84–7
stitchwort 176–9
strawberry 90
string of pearls 170
strobili 73
sunflower 27, 127, 182
sweet pea 198, *199*
sweet potato 45
sweet woodruff 79
Swiss cheese plant 35, 118
sycamore 7, 8–11
sycamore maple 8–11
symbiosis 187

T

tall buttercup 150–3
tansy ragwort 108–11
Taraxacum officinale (dandelion) 7,
   170, 180–3
tares 196–9
tarragon 30
teasle 58–61
thistle 54–7
thistledown 170
Thompson, Ken 149
thyme 127
tobacco substitute 30
Tolpuddle Martyrs 11
tomato 174
touch-me-not 104–7
tree mallow 122
Trifolium (clover) 184–7

Trojan War 14
turions 119
Turkish mad honey 160
twitch 62–5
Tyria jacobaeae (cinnabar moth)
   110–11, 170–1

U

Umbelliferae family, *see Apiaceae*
   family
The Unofficial Countryside (Mabey)
   6
Urtica dioica (stinging nettle)
   188–91
Urticaceae family 113, 168, 188–91

V

Velcro 24, 27, 79
Veronica 'Shirley Blue' 195
Veronica (speedwell) 192–5
verticillasters 140
vetch 76, 196–9
Vicia faba (broad bean) 198
Vicia sativa (common vetch) 196–9
Vicia (vetch) 196–9

W

wall speedwell 192–5
wallflower 49
Waltham Place 45
water aven 90
water lentil 119
watercress 46
waterlily 75
wavy bittercress 49
"weed is a plant in the wrong place"
   principle 103

Weeds Act (1959) 56
Welsh poppy (pani Cymraeg)
   128–31
'whistleweed,' *see* couch grass
white clover 184–7
white deadnettle 112–15
White Garden 67
white herb robert 87
white man's foot, *see* plantain
white willowherb 67
wild arum 32–5
wild daisies 38, *38*
wild teasle 58–61
wild thistles 54–7
Wildlife and Countryside Act
   (1981) 98, 106, 156
willow *67*
willowherb 66–9
winter weeds 22, 114, 178
winterweed 176–9
wood avens 88–91
wood rush 86
woodruff 79
woody nightshade 172–5
Wordsworth, William 75
wormwood 30

Y

yarrow 7, 12–15, *199*
yellow corydalis 142–5
yellow fumitory 142–5

Credits

The publishers would like to thank the following sources for their kind permission to reproduce the pictures in this book.

Illustrations © RHS with the exception of the following:

Akg-Images: Florilegius 196

Alamy: 510 Collection 64; /Album 18, 80, 142, 166; /Artokloro 47; /Bilswissediton, Ltd & Co. KG 24-25, 83; /Chronicle 33; /Florilegius 28, 36, 128, 171; /Hamza Khan 42, 163; /Historical image collection by Bildagentur-online 71, 109; /Interfoto 146; /Jimlop Collection 123; /Library Book Collection 117; /Old Photos 2, 77;/Utcon Collection 168

Bayerische StaatsBiliothek, Germany: 53, 61

BioLib.de: 29, 48, 63, 69, 78, 99, 126, 138, 147, 185, 191

Bibliothèque de l'Université de Strasbourg, France: 144

Bridgeman Images: 100, 199; /Florilegius 118 left; /Photo © Liszt Collection 16-17; /The Stapleton Collection 180

Geheugenvannderland.nl, Amsterdam, The Netherlands 182

Getty Images: Universal History Archive 193

Harvard University Botany Libraries, Cambridge, U.S.A: 96

Missouri Botanical Garden, St. Louis, U.S.A. : 2 bottom left, 15, 22, 39, 50-51, 58, 85, 88, 91, 94, 101, 104, 118 right, 121 right, 123, 140, 155, 183

New York Botanical Garden, U.S.A: 83, 112, 145, 188

Public Domain: 195

Real Jardín Botánico, Madrid, Spain: 8-9, 10, 12-13, 20, 31, 55, 73, 93, 120 left, 186

Royal Library Copenhagen, Denmark: 148

Smithsonian Institute, Washington, D.C., U.S.A: 34, 66-67, 137, 139, 150

Société Nationale d'Horticulture de France, Paris, France: 41

Stellaria media Museum Fieldiana: 179

University of Illinois, U.S.A: 112, 194

Every effort has been made to acknowledge correctly and contact the source and/or copyright holder of each picture and Welbeck Publishing apologizes for any unintentional errors or omissions, which will be corrected in future editions.

About the RHS

The Royal Horticultural Society is Britain's premier gardening charity, promoting horticulture and helping gardeners by providing inspiration through its shows, gardens and expertise. Membership of the RHS brings many benefits to anyone interested in gardening, whatever their level of skill. Membership subscriptions represent a vital element of the Society's funding. To find out more about becoming a member, please visit our website, www.rhs.org.uk.

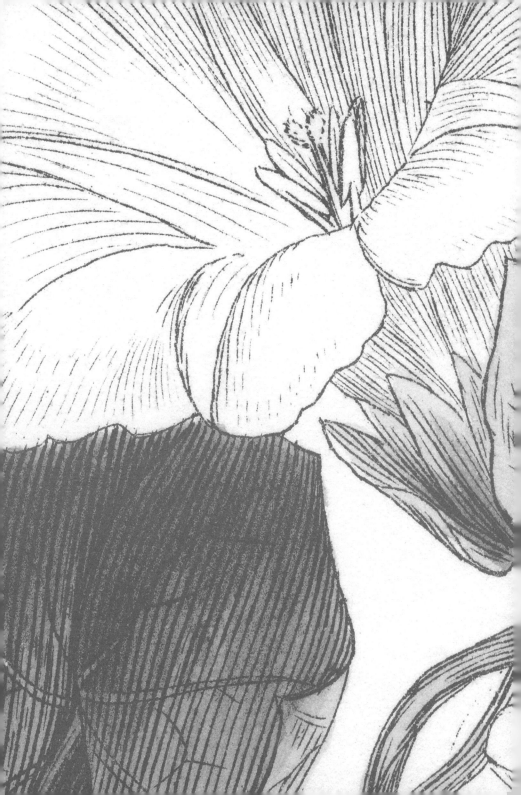